# The World is Crucifixion
# Radical Christian Preaching, Year C

# Intersections
## Theology and the Church in a World Come of Age

Series Editor, Rev. Dr. Christopher Rodkey
*St. Paul's United Church of Christ, Dallastown, PA*

## Advisory Board

Dr. Dan Boscaljon
*The University of Iowa, Iowa City, Iowa*

Rev. James Ellis, III
*Peace Fellowship Church, Washington, DC*

Rev. Dr. Kristina Lizardy-Hajbi
*Center for Research, Analytics, and Data,
United Church of Christ, Aurora, CO*

Rev. Bromleigh McCleneghan
*Union Church of Hillsdale, United Church of Christ, Hillsdale, IL*

Rev. Joshua Patty
*Eastgate Presbyterian Church, Independence, MO*

Rev. Dr. Robert Saler
*Christian Theological Seminary, Indianapolis, IN*

Rev. Dr. Phil Snider
*Brentwood Christian Church, Springfield, MO*

Rev. Dr. John Vest
*Union Presbyterian Seminary, Richmond, VA*

# The World is Crucifixion
# Radical Christian Preaching, Year C

Christopher D. Rodkey

Noesis Press
Aurora, Colorado

Copyright © 2016 Christopher D. Rodkey. All rights reserved. No part of this book may be reproduced, stored in an information retrieval system, or transcribed, in any form or by any means—electronic, digital, mechanical, photocopying, recording, or otherwise—without the express written permission of the publisher.

Library of Congress Cataloging-in-publication data

Names: Rodkey, Christopher D. (Christopher Demuth), author.
Title: The world is crucifixion : radical Christian preaching, Year C / Christopher D. Rodkey.
Description: Aurora, Colorado : The Davies Group, Publishers, 2016. | Series: Intersections: theology and the church in a world come of age | Includes bibliographical references and index.
Identifiers: LCCN 2016002796 | ISBN 9781934542545 (pbk. : alk. paper)
Subjects: LCSH: Church year sermons. | Common lectionary (1992). Year C. | Sermons, American--21st century. | Postmodernism--Religious aspects--Christianity.
Classification: LCC BV4253 .R575 2016 | DDC 252/.058--dc23
LC record available at http://lccn.loc.gov/2016002796

The Scripture quotations contained herein are from the New Revised Standard Version Bible, copyright © 1989 by the Division of Christian Education of the National Council of the Churches in Christ of the U.S.A., and are used with permission. All rights reserved.

Scripture taken from *The Message*. Copyright © 1993, 1994, 1995, 1996, 2000, 2001, 2002. Used with permission of NavPress Publishing Group.

Scripture quotations noted CEB are taken from the Common English Bible, copyright 2011. Used by permission. All rights reserved.

Scripture taken from the NEW AMERICAN STANDARD BIBLE®, Copyright © 1960, 1962, 1963, 1968, 1971, 1972, 1973, 1975, 1977, 1995 by the Lockman Foundation. Used by permission.

Qur'an quotation taken from *The Koran Handbook: An Annotated Translation* by Nicolas Starkovsky. © 2005 Algora Publishing. Used by permission.

Revised Common Lectionary copyright © 1992 Consultation on Common Texts. Used by permission.

# Contents

Foreword by Katharine Sarah Moody vii
Introduction xi

## The Seasons of Advent and Epiphany

1. Is There a God after 9/11? (Advent 1)   3
2. The Joy of Circumcision (Advent 2)   9
3. John the Baptist's Dirty Joke (Advent 3)   17
4. What to Expect When You're Expecting (Advent 4)   25
5. Palm Sunday in December (The Nativity & Christmas Eve)   29
6. Come, Lord Jesus (Feast Day of St. John)   35
7. Crib Notes from Bethlehem (Holy Name of Jesus)   41
8. Coyote Gospel (Baptism of the Lord)   43
9. When Atheists Come for Pizza (Epiphany 5)   49

## The Seasons of Lent and Eastertide

10. Why I Should Be Pope (Lent 1)   55
11. Smelling Like Pig Slop and Loose Women (Lent 4)   63
12. The Resurrectionist (Lent 5)   73
13. How We Kill God (Lent 5, RCL)   81
14. The World is Crucifixion (Lent 6)   93
15. Some Gods Must Die (Easter Vigil)   97
16. I Believe in the Insurrection! (Easter)   105
17. Open Hearts, Open Minds, Rigor Mortis (Easter 6)   113

## Pentecost and the Season after Pentecost

18. A History of Missing the Big Point: Is 160 Years Enough? (Pentecost)   121
19. Blessed Necromancy (Proper 5)   127
20. The Courage to Blaspheme (Proper 10)   133
21. Boldly Prepared for 1950? (Proper 15)   141
22. Why You Should Work on the Sabbath (Proper 16)   147
23. Huge Rummage Sale! (Proper 18)   153

| | | |
|---|---|---|
| 24 | Lessons from the Grocery Store (Proper 20) | 159 |
| 25 | You Can Take It with You! (Proper 21) | 165 |
| 26 | Judas Priest! (Reign of Christ) | 171 |
| 27 | How Christian is Thanksgiving? (Thanksgiving Day) | 177 |

Afterword by Carl Raschke     183

Notes     193

# Foreword

*Do we still hear nothing of the grave-diggers who are burying God? Do we still smell nothing of the divine decomposition?*
—Friedrich Nietzsche, *The Gay Science*[1]

*I am about to do a new thing: now it springs forth, do you not perceive it?*
—Isaiah[2]

In the nineteenth century, Nietzsche observed that belief in the Christian God had become unbelievable. The great atheist critics of Christianity and of Christendom had developed their theories of religion, criticising it as a delusional fantasy about the fulfillment of suppressed desires (Freud), an ideological mask disguising and distorting our real material conditions (Marx), and an instrument of our drive to dominate others (Nietzsche).

God was dead and decomposing.

And still we don't yet fully perceive it.

The death of divinity is too difficult to comprehend, even for the atheists who don't believe in God, since the religious idea of some form of intentionality or agency amidst the ambiguity and antipathy of the impersonal and indifferent world in which we find ourselves lives on in secular post-Christian notions like fate and destiny.

But to announce the death of an infinitely intelligent and intentional supernatural or metaphysical force or entity—the omniscient and omnipotent creator of an ordered universe who has a personal interest in and plan for each of us, who exists beyond but miraculously intervenes in space and time, and whose love and goodness promises a continuation of life after our death—is also to announce the death of any objective God's eye perspective on, transcendent source of or ultimate justification for absolute meaning, purpose, value, truth or telos, of any universal principle, pattern or providence governing the universe and our place in it.

And yet both modern western monotheisms and many modern atheisms continue to make what can be seen as the religious move of denying that it is possible to make sense of our world or to act justly in it without detecting some form of either theistic or atheistic providential agency within it.

Nietzsche's madman remains prophetic, for both theists and atheists. *His message of God's death still comes too early for us.*

But some twentieth and twenty-first century theologians and philosophers have attempted to think through what the death of God might mean for the future of theology, philosophy of religion and religious practice.

The religious and philosophical heritage of a diverse but loosely associated cluster of theologies can be traced back to a range of readings of the death of God, in which the relationship between divinity and death is understood differently by different thinkers. They have asked how religious discourse and practice might be transformed not only by the proclamation of the death of God that can be found within the Christian narrative of God's death on the Cross but also by a passage *through* this death. For the death of God is the death of dogmatic assertions not only of the existence but also of the non-existence of God. The death of God implies *the death of the death of God*, paving the way for a radical theological rethinking or un-thinking of God from within religion as it too is radically reconceived.

For some, however, the death of God functions as little more than a way of keeping God and their faith in God safe. In modernity, God was subject to some killer secular critiques. However, that was not *our* God. That God does not exist; He is dead. But in our *post*-modern, *post*-secular era, the idea of God comes back to life. He is risen indeed! We make use of atheistic critiques of religion *insofar* as they repeat the biblical critique of idols. For these critiques only hold in relation to the God of modern theology. *Ours* is the God beyond that God. The death of (only a certain human conception of) God enables us to discover the God beyond religious idolatry and a faith beyond religious ideology.

But for others, the death of God means even the death of this God beyond God. That God existed once, but does so no more. That transcendent God, existing outside space and time, poured itself out into the immanence of the world at Creation, Christ at the Incarnation, and the Spirit at the Crucifixion and Resurrection. Through a continuing process of self-emptying, self-negation and self-realisation, God moves in, through and as the unfolding of human history. This downward and forward movement is the becoming God of God.

*This* is the new thing that God is doing. If we are perceptive, we will smell it; the rotting remains of the dead God are to be found here – *in* the world. *We* are the body of the Resurrected Christ. After the death of God, theological discourse and religious practice locates the divine wholly within time and space. *This* is The Good News of Christ Crucified that Saint Paul enjoins Christians to preach.

\* \* \*

I met Chris at the first Subverting the Norm conference in October 2010, when he and his colleague Jeff Robbins presented a paper in which they lamented how so-called postmodern, death-of-God and other radical theologies tend to be insufficiently ecclesial and insufficiently political.

The Subverting the Norm conference series brings together theologians, philosophers, church leaders and lay practitioners to explore the possibilities that postmodern theologies (broadly construed) might offer the churches. My research interests lie at the intersection of continental philosophy of religion, radical theology and religious practice; Chris works at this interface. He reminds us that the roles of radical theologian and pastor are not mutually exclusive and might each enrich the other.

The collection of sermons in which you are about to immerse yourself illustrates a convergence of radical theology and the proclamation of faith, in which Preaching Christ Crucified means announcing the becoming God of God through the on-going process of the death of God in human history.

God is dead and decomposing.

But perhaps we don't yet fully perceive it still.

For, if it is to be truly radical, preaching the death of God must prevent us from making the religious move of detecting in what happens supernatural and/or providential agency.

Once what has happened has happened, do we discern in these happenings the *necessary* becoming of God, such that what has come to be is perceived to *always have been coming* and we can rest assured that what is *supposed to come will come*?

Or, as radical theologian John D. Caputo suggests, might we perceive in the historical accidents that happen the *accidental* becoming of God, such that the responsibility for the future is then turned onto *us*?[3]

While the universe may be indifferent, we should not be. Our response to what happens, to what happens to us and to what we make happen, to what has come to be and to what is calling from the future *to come to be*, is our responsibility. But we should perceive in such a responsibility a radical risk rather than a reliable result.

— Katharine Sarah Moody

# Introduction

## Preaching Christ Crucified: Not Evading Nietzsche

*Perhaps the point that I most relish from the death of God controversy is one identifying the death of God theologian as the little boy declaring that the emperor has no clothes, something everyone knows but only the little boy will say out loud. This is actually a profound point even if we appear wholly closed to it. Why are we so closed? And is this true even of the wise ones among us?*
—Thomas J. J. Altizer[1]

*The theology of the Cross is not a theory—it is the reality of Christian life. To live in the belief in Jesus Christ . . . implies daily sacrifice, implies suffering. Christianity is not the easy road; it is, rather, a difficult climb, but one illuminated by the light of Christ and by the great hope that is born of him. Saint Augustine says that Christians are not spared suffering, indeed they must suffer a little more, because to live the faith expresses the courage to face in greater depth the problems that life and history present. But only in this way, through the experience of suffering, can we know life in its profundity, in its beauty, in the great hope born from Christ crucified and risen again.*
—Pope Benedict XVI[2]

*[A]s Jesus himself illustrates under his own circumstances, you do theology not against the background of the death of God but in spite of it, that is, by not domesticating it and not forgetting that no one uses language with impunity any more than one can see God and live.*
—Gabriel Vahanian[3]

In the first volume of my series on radical sermons, *Too Good to Be True*,[4] I proposed that one of the primary themes of radical Christian preaching is the engagement with the idea, symbol, or trope of the death of God. Specifically, I suggested that "radical Christian preaching must declare the Good News of the death of God as the basis of an incarnational faith," and, as such, quoting St. Paul in 1 Corinthians 1:23, this preaching "preaches Christ crucified." One might ask: how does one bring these two primary images—the death of God and preaching Christ crucified—together, since Friedrich Nietzsche and St. Paul are typically understood as opposed, or at least contrary, to each other?

Anyone who has spent any effort reading Nietzsche's works knows that while Nietzsche had a strong distaste for Christianity, he also understood the greatest figures of this epoch of history to be intellectually entangled with Christianity: Jesus, Martin Luther, and, of course, Nietzsche. St. Paul, on the other hand, was for Nietzsche the single most implicated historical figure who made the religion of Jesus tragically its opposite. While scholars since Nietzsche's death have affirmed that the theological program of Paul was different than Jesus' own agenda, and scholars have since similarly acknowledged the tensions between Paul and the other early Apostles, I propose that the answer for radical theology is *not* to reject Paul for Nietzsche. To take Nietzsche's bait is to follow the color-coded error of liberalism or neo-liberalism, as evidenced by the Jesus Seminar. Rather, the radical project is to work *between* the tensions of Nietzsche and Paul.

It is not a completely hyperbolic claim to state that all humane academic disciplines, from literary criticism to psychology, have spent the past century responding in some way to Nietzsche. Yet at the same time many English-speaking philosophers practice their particular kind of philosophy for the sole purpose of evading any possible encounter with Nietzsche. Theology is no different from other disciplines in this regard, with the exception that theology holds a special place in Nietzsche's own ecology as one of the central disciplines that must work through the new age of the death of God. My suspicion is that Nietzsche's desire was not to kill theology or wish its demise, but rather theology survive by changing. No longer a mouthpiece for principalities, powers, and spiritual wickednesses in high places, theology must in this new age oppose the ethical systems of the "beasts of burden" and the "lions." If theology can change, it may be worth saving. Otherwise, for Nietzsche, theology—and with it, all of its expressions, including and especially the church—has no value in the coming age.

When I was a student at the University of Chicago Divinity School, the ministerial students invited Hans-Dieter Betz to give a talk about his role as a clergyman and scholar. As a distinguished, internationally-respected interpreter of the Bible, one of the most memorable things he said to our small group of seminarians on that day was that his entire scholarly project could be understood as being a response to Nietzsche, and that one cannot underestimate the impact of Nietzsche upon European clergy of his generation.

How different times have changed, when many seminaries are graduating ministerial candidates who have never read Nietzsche, let alone Luther or Augustine! In fact, it would appear at times that theology, as a discipline, a *discipline in exile,* is often found in a self-imposed exile for the purpose of *evading Nietzsche.* Christian theology may be, then, today evaluated in categorical manner whether or not the theologian, the theologian's work, or the preacher in her preaching has engaged or is engaging Nietzsche and Nietzschean ideas.

Perhaps our question to the academic theologian or preacher is *whether her theology is hiding from Nietzsche.* It is not coincidental that many "evangelical" or conservative Christians perform their theological tasks as literal readings of other theologians who creatively recant narrow readings of Calvin, Wesley, and

*The Fundamentals.* Liberalism, similarly, elevates Jesus Seminar foundationalism, hiding behind archeological and literary theories which may acknowledge Nietzsche's skepticism of St. Paul, but typically reduce Christ to a philosopher, political rebel, or Buddha who is not necessarily the full and total incarnation, or *kenosis,* of God. Both *evade* Nietzsche's madman-question—*Whither is God?*—with their own modernistic approaches to religion; in both cases God is surely 'up there,' distant, aloof, obfuscating, and while allowing for acts of civil courageousness, this God ultimately demands complicit passivity of 'His' adherents.

In Paul's writings we find the origins of many primary radical theological themes, such as kenosis and an understanding of history as apocalypse. In Philippians 2, Paul describes, perhaps using an early baptismal hymn, the incarnation of Christ as a *kenosis,* a "pouring out" of Spirit into flesh. Specifically, God is described as *"eauton ekenosen,"* that is, *emptying himself* into Jesus Christ (Philippians 2:7). This term, *kenosis,* occurs elsewhere in the New Testament: 1 Corinthians 9:15 uses the word to mean to render void or invalid; in a passive form *kenosis* is used to mean to lose justification in 1 Corinthians 1:17 and Romans 4:14, and *kenosis* is similarly employed in 2 Corinthians 9:3. Paul's use of *kenosis* in Philippians reveals an important characteristic about the relationship between God and Jesus, namely, that this relationship is a motion of God *emptying Godself* into the incarnation of the Christ. As radical theologian Thomas J. J. Altizer observes, this kenotic movement of the Divine is "of Eternity becoming, or of the sacred becoming profane."[5]

This is to say that a Christology which takes kenosis seriously understands God working in history through a process of self-negation: God dies into Christ. God in Christ dies on the cross. Flesh is exalted with Spirit in the resurrection of Jesus. The Holy Spirit pours out into "all flesh"[6] on the Day of Pentecost. Today ecclesiologists often speak of an "incarnational" approach to church, but what is meant by "incarnation" is usually a sense of intimacy. A fully incarnational approach to the church is one that recognizes the *enfleshed immanence* of God in the presence of the gathered assembly, and realizing that to speak of God "up there," of transcendence, can only be genuine when it causes us "down here" to self-transcend, to *break the absolute hymen*[7] between sacred and secular, to reverse the world from beginning to end. The poor, meek, widowed: the *reversal* of alpha and omega.

There could be no more offensive faith to this world, or its Christian expressions, than an authentic and radical proclamation of the death of God, of radical theology. *Preaching Christ crucified*, as Paul declares in 1 Corinthians 1:23, invokes not only the abject offense of the symbol of God's death by human hands, but eucharistically ingesting and bearing the cross for others as our kingdom-work toward a full parousia, second coming. If Pentecost is the pouring out of Spirit into all flesh, the work of parousia has only begun. *Pentecost-ing*, preaching Christ crucified, is speaking to or with an audience without condescension but with a *charge*: the Kingdom of God is perpetually *not-yet*, but yet not a reality of God "not afar off," to cite William Blake.[8] The charge and challenge is for the enfleshed Godhead—that is, *us*—as a whole to bear the cross for Godself; that is, to evoke actual self-sacrifice, to pour ourselves out into the world awaiting the sanctification of our secularized and secularizing kenosis.

I believe that if humanity really wanted to solve the problems of the world, we could. As Slavoj Žižek so poignantly repeats throughout his work, those of us predisposed toward neoliberalism are caught up in false apocalypticism. We like movies where we can detonate bombs to destroy threatening meteors, and believe we can fix natural aspects of global warming, but yet we cannot seem to figure out how to pay teachers to educate children. Nor can we in the United States figure out how to ensure that young people go to bed with enough to eat and with a confidence of safety in their homes. These realities do not only stem from pure ideology, but are rooted in Satanic laziness and religious complicity: *passivity*. If the so-called First World, which is really the One-Third World, really wanted to begin to solve the problems of, for example, Africa—*if we really wanted to do it*—we could do it. And by "we" I do not simply mean to imply a colonializing savior approach to American theology, but I mean *we* as a unified, member-ed "GloboChrist" community. More could be said about this, and obviously, I am being very selective and narrow in my choices of examples.

Yet my point remains: if our Christian faith is one of transfiguration, one of self-transcendence, our faith can move mountains.[9] If Godhead can speak the world into existence, if Christ can heal and defeat death, if the Spirit can pour liberally upon All Flesh, then the very human problems of this world may be solved. The human problems which remain to be solved are summarized in the beatitudes.[10] They must be our agenda as radical preachers, and the Word proclaimed must be the charge of the Word enfleshed.

## Nietzschean Hermeneutics

This book of sermons follows the Revised Common Lectionary, Year C. Most of these sermons have been preached at Zion "Goshert's" United Church of Christ (Lebanon, PA) and St. Paul's United Church of Christ (Dallastown, PA); others were preached at Community UCC (Mountain Lakes, NJ) and a myriad of other places where I have been a guest preacher. Like its previous volume, *Too Good to be True*, this book, *The World is Crucifixion*, is not meant to be a complete preaching guide but a glimpse and guide into the work of radical Christian preaching. Sometimes the images are funny, sometimes disturbing, sometimes closely exegetical. I have selected the sermons in this volume because of the *reversal* invoked in their texts. That is, I intend in the sermons to occur a fundamental *reversal* or a charge for reversal. The task of preaching here is not always purely instructional, but more often commissioning, *ordaining* its audience for the work of *reversals*.

What do I mean by "reversal"? Mary Daly charged that the evil, or *necrophilial* evil, of Christendom is the "realm of reversals of the fathers."[11] For her, Christianity at its patriarchal worst, actively identified ideas as their opposites: death equates eternal life; pro-life really means pro-death; pro-family means misanthropy; the "moral majority" rests upon a base nihilism. While Daly no longer has time for Christianity, for we who choose to remain we recognize that Jesus himself attempted to evoke a tremendous reversal of religion, exposing the death-lusting reversals of the Temple, and the hypocrisy of popular religion. Jesus' parables similarly invoke a *parabolic* reversal: the irony of the stories are not just unexpected plot resolutions but spiritual and ethical lessons which challenge the entire political and religious systems of his day.

Sometimes in our preaching we must dissect the language and contexts to expose the actual reversal, and sometimes we need to expose how the church has domesticated the message or dissected the radical message plainly present in scripture. This is to say, radical preaching demands a *Nietzschean hermeneutic*. If Jesus, for Nietzsche, is the greatest failure of our epoch of history, the failure is not upon Jesus himself but is a condemnation of the church for not taking him seriously, reducing his message to a reversal of its actual meaning, creating a religion which reflects the religiosity against which Jesus himself rebelled.

Radical preaching, then, is an act of *reversing* the reversals, of exposing and illuminating the reversals which need to be *reversed*. Telling stories, reciting songs and poetry, interpreting sacred texts which aid and inspire the *reversal* of reversals. The act of reversing reversals, what Mary Daly calls "Spinning," is not always consistent, not always intellectually clean, not always politically correct, and is never socially polite.[12] Preaching calls forth and enacts these reversals, and hopes to inspire others to similarly decenter, sublimate, kenote, Spin, *reverse*.

∗ ∗ ∗

It is my intention that this book be enjoyed by Christians seeking sermons and by clergy looking for ideas for their preaching. Good preaching occurs in a multi-ocular environment, where inspiration comes from television, film, music, games, comics, newspapers, digital media, social networking, sports, relationships, and spiritual disciplines. I am particularly indebted to Swanson's *Provoking the Gospel*,[13] the United Church of Christ's SAMUEL preaching resource,[14] and the online Girardian Commentary on the Lectionary.[15] Theologically, these sermons are preached along with radical theologians who have influenced my life and work: Thomas Altizer, Gabriel Vahanian, René Girard, Mary Daly, Peter Rollins, and Carl Raschke.

Preaching occurs from the contexts of the preachers' clouds of witnesses. First, I would like to thank my congregation, St. Paul's United Church of Christ, in Dallastown, Pennsylvania, and our secretary, Ms. Chris Raffensburger, for their professional support. Similarly, my colleagues and students at Lebanon Valley College, Penn State York, Lexington Theological Seminary, and York College of Pennsylvania are to be thanked for research and travel support, feedback, and listening to many of the ideas in the classroom. My colleagues John Vest, Josh Patty, Phil Snider, Jeff Robbins, and my friend Ms. Lyn Ridgeway have always been deeply supportive of my work. The Rev. Dr. Daniel Peterson's recommendations have been especially helpful in my revision of the text. Special thanks to Dr. Victor Taylor and Mr. James K. Davies for supporting the fruition of this book, and to Carl Raschke and Katharine Sara Moody for contributing to the book. A few sermons have been previewed on the online community, *An und für sich*[16] and I thank Adam Kotsko and Brad Johnson for their invitation to continue as part of that blog.

My family—Traci, Christian, Annaliese, Scarlett, and Gabriel—are always to be celebrated by me for tolerating my theological ministry and pastoral calling, especially when that call takes me away from them for hours or days at a time.

Christopher D. Rodkey<br>
Dallastown, Pennsylvania<br>
November 21, 2014<br>
Memorial of the Presentation of Mary

The Seasons of Advent and Epiphany

# 2 THE WORLD IS CRUCIFIXION

## Is There a God after 9/11?
### (Advent 1)
### Jeremiah 33:14–16; Luke 21:25–36

How appropriate to begin a new liturgical season, a new liturgical year, with a vision of The End, an apocalyptic vision of Jesus, remembering, of course, that the word *apocalypse* means "unveiling." Jesus is unveiling some hidden truth or hidden knowledge, or exposing something new that was previously buried.

Too often the way we think about the apocalypse is something that is far off in the future, but the Bible means something very different than this, that the apocalypse is something always just about to happen, always around the corner, always immediate. To read, for example, the epistles of Paul in any other way than with the apocalypse just about to happen is a false interpretation. For the earliest Christians the now is a liminal space between the past and the second coming of Christ.

One of my favorite jokes about the apocalypse is that Jesus came back and told everyone that they had exactly three weeks to prepare for the end of the world. So folks came to church *en masse,* and people were telling the pastor everything they were doing to get ready. The pastor kept telling everyone to ask for forgiveness, to repent, and to mend ties with family members they had fallen out with.

So one guy told the pastor in passing that he decided to move in with his mother-in-law for the remaining three weeks before the coming apocalypse. The pastor said, "That's a really sweet gesture, I am really glad you're taking seriously the message I've been giving to heal ties."

And the guy looked at him funny, and said, "No, living with my mother-in-law for these three weeks will make those three weeks feel like an eternity!"

\* \* \*

Back to the Bible: the prophet Jeremiah makes the claim that "the days are surely coming . . . when I will fulfill the promise I made to the house of Israel and the house of Judah. In those days and at that time I will cause a righteous Branch to spring up for David; and he shall execute justice and righteousness in the land. In those days Judah will be saved and Jerusalem will live in safety. And this is the name by which it will be called: 'The Lord is our righteousness.'"

Imagine how these words of the prophet Jeremiah would have been heard during the time in which they were probably written—after the first temple was destroyed and the Jews were taken into captivity, the temple as the home of God was destroyed and along with it the city, and again with all of this destruction was the morale and will of the people.

The words of the prophet were hopeful words coming from within a deep crisis. But the language of hope here is worth pointing out. The prophet does not say "I told you so," or at least not here he does not; and the prophet does not say "we will get our revenge." The language of the prophet—the Word of God—is the language of *righteousness*: trusting in God will make the paths straight and will provide redemption to the people, but *not* of violence and revenge. The redemption is that God is still with them *through* the destruction, *through* all of the death and genocide, and *in the face* of great uncertainty. Those who believed that God literally lives in the inner chamber of the Temple are going to have to get over their literalisms and get over their old ways and rethink God anew and alive in our time, or the only other remaining option is to declare openly that God is dead, and that God remains dead.

The implication here is that those who hold onto the old ways have killed, and are killing God, by quite literally keeping God in the box—that is, keeping God inside of the inner chamber of the Temple now destroyed—*keeping God in the box* especially in a time of crisis. For the prophet God is not only alive but, that is, God will offer redemption in the form of justice: righteousness and safety.

Here redemption is the key word of God's promise made to those in crisis; and if we jump ahead a few hundred years to our Jesus story from the Gospel of Luke this morning we hear Jesus speaking apocalyptically. He says: "There will be signs in the sun, the moon, and the stars, and on the earth distress among nations confused by the roaring of the sea and the waves. People will faint from fear and foreboding of what is coming upon the world, for the powers of the heavens will be shaken. Then they will see 'the Son of Man coming in a cloud' with power and great glory. Now when these things begin to take place, stand up and raise your heads, *because your redemption is drawing near."* To repeat: here we encounter that word "redemption" from the prophet Jeremiah again. We can talk a lot about the term "redemption," but what does it mean?

To redeem is to turn something in or exchange, but redemption in the ancient world emphasized the idea of exchanging something for a debt with the word "redemption." Usually a redemption was what was paid to release a slave or servant from servitude or bondage, or in the case of the Jews now deported from their land and into captivity in Babylon, redemption is the price God will pay to buy them out of their exile.

So if the coming promise of God in crisis is not of revenge, but of redemption, and the messiah speaks that our redemption is coming near, what could Jesus mean by all of this? We know from going to Sunday school that the answer to nearly every question is "Jesus"—so if Jesus is our redeemer, what is he freeing us from exactly? The answer to this is complicated and the answer is usually "sin," but the fact is that beyond sin, Jesus is saving us from ourselves and those institutions and forces and powers and spiritual wickednesses that hold us back from being genuine with ourselves and each other.

So this is why Jesus uses the kind of language that he does here: that there will be signs in the sun and in the moon, and the stars, and roaring of the sea and waves. Something is coming that will shake the very foundations that will force us to rethink and force us to reform everything we know. The heavens and the earth are going to be breeched, and shatter, and crumble, until all that we could possibly know is that God is with us, and God has never left us. So that when we feel claustrophobic from all sides of the world closing in on us, we may have faith and trust that God is bigger than all of this. When people backbite you and bear false witness against you, even when the gossip and lies have significant consequences, our faith is that God will deliver not revenge, but righteousness, and that our redemption is being freed from the captivities imposed upon us by ourselves and by others.

* * *

Recently I had a conversation with a student who told me that she could not believe in God because of 9/11. After 9/11, there could be no God because God would never allow anything that awful to happen, and that God is not the answer to the problem of 9/11. It would seem that belief in God was in fact the cause of the terrorist acts of 9/11.

If with me you have also witnessed the past years' earthquakes, tornados, hurricanes, floods, typhoons and super-typhoons, we may ask honestly whether "God" is the answer to the problem of natural disaster? Is Jesus the answer to this problem of total destruction? This is of course the same question posed to us by the prophet Jeremiah, but we should remember that the Bible never says that you will get a new house, and the Bible never says that life will always be perfect, and the Bible makes no promise that you will never suffer, but only that God's redemption is coming.

So the answer to the question of the student who could not believe in God after 9/11 is that *the only possible God she is looking to believe in,* a God who is there to offer simple answers to difficult questions, *is a God that never existed, never will exist, and is not the God of scripture.* The God of scripture does not necessarily demand belief from us, but is actually *luring* us to *trust* the God who makes promises of redemption. The Good News is not that a God will fix our problems, even when our problems involve the destruction of the city—as it was in the year 500 BC as it is in 2015 AD—but that God will make things right in the future. The Bible says, "days are surly coming," that is to say, *trust me.*

With all of this in mind, we should review the end of Jesus' teaching for us today: "Be on guard so that your hearts are not weighed down with dissipation and drunkenness and the worries of this life, and that day catch you unexpectedly, like a trap. For it will come upon all who live on the face of the whole earth. Be alert at all times, praying that you may have the strength to escape all these things that will take place, and to stand before the Son of Man."

God made a promise to send a messiah. God made a promise that he would not only be with his people, but God more radically makes good on his promise to come and live with us and to take on the flesh of humanity. And God died a human death to make good on that promise. God made a promise that the "days are surely coming" that our redemption will be made. What we need to do in response is that we need to trust that God makes good on his promises, as he always does. By taking on flesh and death, God knows our suffering. And knowing that suffering, God puts a gentle hand on our shoulders in moments of despair, whispering a reminder: "*trust me.*"

And by trusting in God, we realize that we live in a world that is not yet redeemed, a world that is not yet saved, and a world not yet having realized the fullness of God. We need to trust, and teach others to trust. How do we do this? When we see the destruction of Staten Island, we donate our *abundances* to someone else's *neediness*. When we see someone in despair on the road, we act as the Good Samaritan. When we see someone in pain, we work, even when the work is hard, toward redemption. It's not just an abstract idea that God will bring his redemption. The Good News is that we can trust in our own redemption as we work to build the trust of God for others.

\* \* \*

As we venture into this season of Advent, the temptation for us is to jump a little too quickly into the celebration of Christmas. Every year Christmas arrives in the stores a little earlier, or at least it seems so to me. *We need to trust the calendar.* Christmas will surely come. December 25 is going to arrive.

But we should trust God more than the calendar. Trusting God in this Advent season is not just reminding excited children that the gifts will be under their trees, but trusting God is, as Jesus says, being on watch: Don't be weighed down with the drunkenness and worries of this life. Don't be ensnared and entrapped by the things of this world that ultimately don't matter. For the coming redemption, to again use Jesus' own words, "*will come* upon all who live on the face of the earth. Be alert at all times, praying that you may have the strength to escape all these things that will take place, and to stand before the Son of Man." Redemption *will come.*

It seemed to me that after 9/11, we as a nation had a tremendous opportunity to open dialogue on a world level about terrorism and violence, and how to turn the other cheek, and how to practice peace. When Christians wage war as revenge, yes, it seems to me that such a religion is a religion not worth believing in. To reject belief in such a God is in fact the proper response. The challenge of our time today, and in the coming year, is to take up the cross of practicing peace and practicing redemption, and rejecting the logic of violence and war and poverty and mass disease and the destruction of cities. If Christianity is to be known as a true religion, and a religion of peace, and of hope, and of Joy (that is, what we say our religion is when we light Advent candles), and of the redemption of the world, we need to take the words of Jesus very seriously—in a way that Christianity has failed to do in the past. We need to open our deaf ears to God's message, saying, *trust me.*

Let us now enter into this advent season with a spirit of trust: trusting that God will redeem us, and practicing that trust in radical and new ways to demonstrate to a world that thirsts for violence, and war, and revenge, that trusting in non-violence, and trusting in peace, and trusting in redemption is how God will be made known to this world, this *hurting world,* that has no conception of the fullness of the truth offered to us in this Good News of Jesus Christ.

## The Joy of Circumcision
(Advent 2)
*Malachi 3:1–4; Romans 3:29–30; Luke 1:59–80, 3:1–6*

Our focus this Sunday is John the Baptist, who as a figure or theme from the Bible is not very Christmas-y but is one of the important elements of Advent, which is the preparation of the world for the coming of Jesus. Sometimes we forget just how important John the Baptist is in the Jesus story, and in the Gospel of Luke, if you read from the very beginning of this book in the Bible, after the first introductory paragraph in chapter 1, the opening of the Gospel is entirely upon John the Baptist and his father, Zechariah, before going back in time to talk about Mary being called by God.

The first part of our story today is the circumcision of John the Baptist. As was Jewish custom, on the eighth day of the boy's life John was taken to be circumcised, which would have also been the time of the announcement of the boy's name. Everyone is astonished when the parents announce to name the baby John, rather than Zechariah or another family name. Like today new parents often choose baby names from other family names, and this was the case back then, but it was highly unusual for a baby of a Jewish priest of stature to be given a name completely outside of the family's tradition. This apparently was such a big deal that Zechariah was unable to speak until he wrote down the words, "His name is John."

So Zechariah, who was temporarily unable to speak, and was part of a highly respected class of Jewish priests, was magically able to speak at the moment of the naming of the newborn child. And then the first words out of his mouth came when he was filled with the Holy Spirit, praising God and prophesying that this little baby boy will be a great prophet who will "prepare his ways." The last line of Zechariah's song of praise sings that the baby boy will "give light to those who sit in darkness and in the shadow of death, to guide our feet into the way of peace."

This is an allusion to the twenty-third Psalm, specifically the line, I am sure many of you know it, "even though I walk through the valley of the shadow of death, I fear no evil"—Zechariah is saying that this baby boy will grow to be a prophet who leads his people out of the darkest valley.

The event of that day, the circumcision of John, happens behind the scenes of the larger scheme of history, and to make sense of why the circumcision of John the Baptist is so important to those who wrote this Gospel down, we have to look ahead in the Gospel of Luke a little bit. The third chapter of John begins by listing all of the tyrants who ruled the world at the time. If you were going to begin to talk about all of the big problems of the world today, you'd start by naming the presidents, kings, and terrorists whose actions have tremendous consequences all over the world, that if they just went away, it would seem, a big part of our problems would also disappear.

What is interesting about this list of names is they all point to events that happened 150 years before, so that by naming all of these leaders, the Gospel writers are pointing toward someone unnamed whose actions led to the then-current political situation which allowed for the names mentioned in the Gospel to be in power. In particular I am referring to Antiochus IV, who instigated a war today called the "Maccabean War." This war, the Maccabean War, happened around 150 B.C. You've all heard of the Jewish holiday called "Hanukkah" that is celebrated around this time of year—Hanukkah is actually the holiday when Jews remember the events of the Maccabean War.

What caused this particular war was that Antiochus IV wanted to force everyone under his rule to worship him above as the highest God, in fact, he called himself Antiochus Epiphanes, which means, "Antiochus, the God Revealed." Most of the groups living within the empire just played along with worshiping the emperor to appease the him, but the Jews refused to revere the Emperor as a god because the Jews knew that even if the claim that the Emperor was God was not serious, it was still sinful and a form of idolatry to render any political leader as God. And furthermore, many Jews were looking in expectation for a coming messiah, who would have been understood by them as *the* God revealed, so they found Antiochus IV's claim to be *the* Revealed God to be quite contradictory to their beliefs, and offensive to their hope for the coming messiah.

When the Jews refused to comply with Antiochus' demands to be worshiped, he lashed out on them. He made it illegal for the Jews to observe the Sabbath and he forbade the practice of circumcision, which was and is the primary way that Jews physically mark their faith upon their flesh. Antiochus' laws did little to stop the Jews, so he went to drastic measures of enforcement. Antiochus issued a decree that if a baby boy was found to have been circumcised, the baby was to be killed in the mother's presence and the baby's corpse was to be tied around the woman's neck until the child's body rotted away. Even though this was no longer the law, they knew that at any time the political winds could change and the men could be identified by this mark on their flesh. And, of course, we knew that this was one way that the Nazis, two thousand years later, would often identify who were the Jews to be taken away for execution—not very long ago.

In our Bible story we have a family of priests gathering for a circumcision, and the father proclaims that the boy is going to "break the dawn from on high, bring light into the valley of the shadow of death, and lead the Jewish people to peace." So this act of circumcision is not just an act of compliance with the Jewish customs and not just seen as a privilege when having a child circumcised not very long ago could lead to terrible punishments, but this act of circumcision is then to be understood to be a revolutionary and subversive ritual, flaunting the *limited* religious freedom that they had at the time, and predicting and predicating a new revolution coming from God—centered upon this little baby boy, whose flesh was being marked and *carved* as being part of the faith, *a subversive and transgressive faith that is against the state, against the Empire.*

\* \* \*

Later we find John the Baptist as an adult wandering in the desert proclaiming baptism as the mark of redemption and salvation, *rather* than circumcision. John preaches, "prepare the way of the Lord, make his paths straight." This is one of the most famous lines of the Gospels, which comes from the words of Isaiah, to prepare the way of the Lord, make his paths straight, the crooked will be made straight, and the rough ways made smooth, and the last line of our Bible reading, "and all flesh shall see the salvation of God."

There's a lot to talk about in these few lines of scripture. If you've ever been to a Jewish home, or at least a home where they are practicing and actively observing the Jewish religion, they have a *mezuzah* hanging up at their doorway. I have a photo of a mezuzah in your bulletin. You'd notice, though, that the mezuzah is always tilted, it's never hung squarely on a home outside of Jerusalem. This is because the Jews believe that only inside of the Temple in Jerusalem is there order in the universe, and the further away you get from the Temple in Jerusalem, to wherever you are now, the more crooked and strange the world is. The mezuzah is a reminder to the Jew of how backwards and imperfect the world is, that no matter how good life might be for me right now, every time I walk into my house I can be reminded that I am living the good life in a crooked world, and I need to be reminded that the ways of being right with God are *not* the ways of being right with the world or other people.

When John the Baptist says that "the crooked shall be made straight and the rough made smooth," he is proclaiming from the wilderness, which would have been in the crooked part of the world, away from Jerusalem, inhabited by people whom the city-dwellers looked down on as being in the cooked part of the universe. John is proclaiming to those who are seen as lower class and of lower status that a cataclysmic event is coming, that when God will enter the world in the coming of the messiah, this entrance is not just the coming of a prophet or a great teacher or someone who will restore Judaism to its rightful place in society, but even more directly: John proclaims God, *Godself*—not a messenger, not a prophet, not a teacher, not a philosopher, but that God, *prepare ye the way*—is coming into the world. And again, it's also important that John preaches these words out in the wilderness, far away from the Temple, and in the crooked part of the Jewish understanding of the universe, signifying that the coming of the messiah into the world is not going to happen as a Jew living in Jerusalem at that time might expect the messiah to come (which would, of course, been in the temple); rather, God himself is coming into this crooked and bent-up countryside to shake the very foundations of what those in the city and those at the center of religious power believe God wants in this world. Those in power and those with wealth looking for God to enter the world through the gates of the temple are going to be *quite surprised* that God will enter this world through the womb of an unwed, teenage mother in a barn, and that this same God will descend further into human flesh and further into the world through a death on the cross.

And beyond this, the message of God through Jesus is quite precisely through the messiah, coming into the crooked part of the world on the boundary of society means that God is not just coming into the world just for a small group of privileged priests inside of the temple—that is, the family of John the Baptist—and not just for all of the Jews, including the poorest ones who live in the wilderness, but that *God comes into the world for the salvation of all of humanity, and not just some of humanity.*

John the Baptist, whose naming and circumcision arrive with a declaration from his prophet father, a priest of the Temple, proclaiming that John would testify to the giving of light and the leading out of the valley of the shadow of death; and *this same John the Baptist*, whose circumcision was seen as a radical act of defiance against the political powers; *and it is this same John the Baptist* is now as an adult found negating and *rendering invalid* the entire idea of circumcision for now and in the future. In other words, the mark of being a member of God's chosen race is no longer being cut in the flesh and is no longer limited to a ritual done only for certain people of a certain race under a very specific and narrow covenant or contract with God; rather, God has come to the world for everyone to be offered a branch on God's family tree. The baptism offered by John is a liberation from old religion and into something entirely new.

This is such a radically different message than traditional Judaism, that we find John the Baptist later preaching his message of repentance and baptism far away from the temple where his father ministered as a priest, in the wilderness, away from the wealthy benefactors of the temple in the boundary area of the countryside: away from the zealots in the temple, and probably away from his own family. But John is preaching that when God comes as the Messiah, the world will be made right again, if only for a little while, and a New Creation will then commence, recalling that the last time the universe was without sin and without evil was at the moment of creation, before Adam and Eve came onto the scene.

Christians understand that the washing that occurs in the baptism demonstrated to us by John the Baptist is a replacement for circumcision. We as Christians don't have to be scarred in the flesh, *but we need to be renewed by and through the Holy Spirit.* We should recall that when God created the earth, he swept over the face of the waters, and split the waters, placing a division in the waters, and spoke forth the land. So too when we remember our baptism and rededicate our baptisms *we become part of this sacred history of creation and ongoing re-creation,* which once required circumcision of us, but now only demands that we live the circumcised life with our heads still wet with baptism.

The Good News is that God does not want us to offer ourselves up as a blood sacrifice by scarring our flesh, but only that we understand that our physical dependence upon water as an element of life to be an analogy and symbol for our spiritual dependence upon baptism. Baptism is what unites us as a community, and baptism is what nourishes us and keeps us alive. *Baptism circumcises and circumscribes* us to the history of the people who are circumcised, that is, the Jews, through the parting of the waters at creation, through the crossing of the Jordan and the Red Sea, through the rainbow-promises given through droplets of water after the flood, through Jonah living in the whale deep in the oceans, and through the promise of the river of life coming down out of heaven—it would seem that water is an important and necessary symbol of our faith.

We may not be a fully circumcised people but we are a Baptized people who understand the Good News that the promises of God and the love of God for this world is not limited to a small group of people but is open to everyone—men and women, rich and poor, powerful and exploited, from the main line to death row and skid row. The God that works through baptism works far more radically than we could possibly imagine.

But for so many of us, when it comes to our faith, we are silent, like Zechariah, and only speak openly about our faith when our children are baptized or when giving eulogies at funerals, or giving prayers at occasional big family meals. It's time for us today to open up our mouths and let the Holy Spirit fill these tongues with fire, that we go out into the world to tell our friends and family not only about the Good News of Advent and Christmas, that God incarnated into the world as a baby 2,000 years ago, but more importantly of the God who incarnates and is continuing to incarnate in our lives now. This is to say: Go from this place and spread the baptism around!

## John the Baptist's Dirty Joke
(Advent 3)
*Luke 3:7–18*

We all know people who think that just because they say that they are "born again," they have something special that makes them better than other people. I consider myself to be "born again," but not "born again" in the way that many evangelical pastors use this language. Not too long ago someone stopped by my door in Lebanon asking me to vote for her for a local election, and she gave me a glossy card with a kind of laughable list of qualifications to run for judge: She had a degree in art, she was endorsed by the local Tea Party, she took a two week class on how to run a courtroom, and finally the card said she was "born again."

I love it when politicians knock on my door, because I like to mess with them.

First, I asked her if she had ever been inside of the county prison, and I said that it would be immoral to vote for anyone to be a judge sending people to a prison she herself has never been inside of. To that she said, but I've never been arrested, so why would I go inside of the county prison?

But second, I asked her why being "born again" made her qualified to be a judge. She said, "Well, I am glad you asked!" And then she told me that because she was born again, she had a higher understanding of the laws of the Old Testament, and believed that Jesus liberates her from the laws and that Jesus is the fulfillment of the law—she kept talking about the "law," you see, because she was running to be a local judge—and that Jesus is her personal Lord and savior, and so on and so forth, *most important to all of this,* she said, *I am a born-again Christian.*

But then I asked again: "What does that have to do with being a judge?"

Then she asked if I was a Christian, and I said, actually, I'm a pastor. And she said of which church, and I said the United Church of Christ. In response, she had this weird look on her face, and said, "oh, well then you don't know what I'm talking about then."

I asked her to explain what she meant. "Our pastor talks about how those in United Church of Christ aren't really Christians. You're not really born again."

I gave her my business card and I invited her to church, and we parted ways.

We all know people who say they're "born again" who think they're better than everyone else, think they've unlocked some secret key to the universe, and that everyone who might think differently from them is definitely wrong. And as I said before, I consider myself "born again," but I also take issue with how many Protestants interpret this phrase and impose their ideas on other people.

In our Gospel reading we find John the Baptist addressing this very same issue directly: Do you think you're better than other people because you got baptized? And John looks directly at the same people he just baptized and swears at them: "You Brood of Vipers!" We should never lose sight that this is first-century swearing; in fact, I like to think of John saying these words in the voice of the actor Samuel L. Jackson, who is known for swearing in his movies (I'm thinking *Snakes on a Plane* here): *You brood of vipers!* Instead of calling them a bunch of S.O.B.'s he called them a bunch of S.O.V.'s: You sons of vipers! Your mother's a snake!

But John's insults go beyond this . . . and this is kind of a PG-13 rated sermon. John says to the newly baptized people who think they're awesome, "Don't keep saying to yourselves that 'Abraham is my ancestor!'" In other words, folks baptized by John were not only claiming to be *both* liberated by the baptism of water and the Spirit by John, and directly descended into the present by their blood ancestor, Abraham. A sense of spiritual lineage in this radical act of baptism is definitely *not* what this is all about.

Here's where it gets a little dirty: John then says, "God is able from *these stones* to raise up children to Abraham. Even now the ax is lying at the foot of the trees; every tree therefore that does not bear fruit is cut down and thrown in the fire." There are many different ways of reading this, but we should think of this as pretty crude language that makes a serious point. The ancestral lineage from Abraham was passed through the semen of the father to the next generation.

So when John says he is going to cut down "these trees," what trees are he talking about? And when he's talking about "these stones," what is John talking about? We need to understand that these are crude, dirty jokes being told by this dirty, smelly guy wearing a thong–the Bible says that all he was wearing was a thong in Matthew 3—so we can assume here that those near to John the Baptist, so close to him that they could smell him *knew exactly what he was talking about here* with "these *trees*," from which the semen of lineage of Abraham is descended, and "these *stones*," out for folks to see.

If we can acknowledge the crudeness and kind of dirtiness of the way John the Baptist is talking here, maybe we can better understand what he's really saying. First, he is saying that spiritual and blood ancestry *of* and *from* Abraham doesn't mean anything in the eyes of God. It doesn't matter whose sperm and whose womb created you (remembering that the spiritual authority of Abraham is passed through semen, but what makes a Jew is Jew by the law is if your mother is a Jew; Jewishness is defined as having come from a Jewish womb), but that what you do in this world is far more important than where you came from. And this is especially true if you claim some sort of spiritual superiority because of who your parents are, or which family you came from, or which high priest circumcised you, or who baptized you—keeping in mind that these words are coming from the man who baptized all of these people, whose own father was an elite priest of the temple in Jerusalem.

So the ax at the root of the tree is John the Baptist's metaphor to say that if you think your ancestral lineage to Abraham, as passed down through the generations through the sexual acts and organs of our fathers, and if the mark of Abraham is circumcised on your sexual organs—*it's time to cut them all off.* Just as Jesus would later say to cut off a hand that is sinning, or to tear out an eye that causes you to sin: if the mark of circumcision on a particular part of your body is causing you to think you're better than others, *it's time to cut that tree down at its roots.* The exact words of scripture are "Even now the ax is lying at the root of the trees; every tree therefore that does not bear good fruit is cut down and thrown into the fire!"

\* \* \*

John then goes on to prophesy about the coming of Jesus: "I baptize you with water, but one who is more powerful than I is coming; I am not worthy to untie his sandals. He will baptize you with the Holy Spirit and with fire. His winnowing fork is in his hand, to clear the threshing-floor and gather wheat into the granary, but the chaff he will burn with an unquenchable fire!"

The problem with the way we usually read these words is the word in Greek for "Winnowing fork." The Greek word for "winnowing fork," is *ptuon,* but *ptuon* really means a winnowing *shovel,* not a fork. Why does this matter? A winnowing fork would have been used in a granary to separate the majority of the wheat from the chaff. A winnowing shovel would have been used for the leftovers, the small pieces left behind.

So why this is so important is that later, in Luke 7, when there is a disagreement between Jesus and John the Baptist about whether there would be fire or redemption, Jesus corrects John, saying in Luke 7:23, "Blessed is he who is not offended in me." In other words, John's prophesy is only fulfilled halfway by Jesus: Jesus offers a message of *redemption and forgiveness* and *hope.* Jesus separates the wheat from the chaff by virtue of those who freely accept the path of the cross or those who do not.

The point being this: Jesus did not come into this world to condemn it—we should remember that this is the line right after John 3:16, which we all know so well: "For God so loved the world, that he gave his only begotten son, that whosoever believes in him should not perish but have everlasting life." This famous line is followed by a clarification that we so often forget, John 3:17: "Indeed, God did not send the Son into the world to condemn the world, but in order that the world might be saved through him."

These words are key here: Jesus did not come to condemn the world, but to save it. John the Baptist believes that Jesus is entering the world to start tearing the world down. Jesus says later, *not so fast*. The message of Jesus will turn this world upside down, and it will make the crooked straight, and the rough path smooth, and open boundaries and doors where they are closed, and Jesus' death will tear the curtain of the temple in two and shake the foundations of the earth, but Jesus' message is one of peace, and it is a message of forgiveness, and redemption, and Jesus' message is of salvation—*not of eternal perishing*.

So, then, the Good News, it would seem, is that while some in our world choose violence, and hatred, and racism, and classism, and all of the -ism's that make the world bad, those who are in Christ, even those who would seem to be left behind when the blessings of this world are handed out, are those working to undo the evils and the violence of this world and are working for peace. Jesus gathers *many* by the winnowing fork, but those who feel like they're left behind, if they are in Christ, they need not worry, that they will be gathered up with the rest of those who live in Christ.

The focus of John might be the fires of hell and the wrath of God waiting to annihilate those who do not comply. The message of Christ is to focus on the free choice and the salvation offered in this free choice. There is still wrath to come in Jesus' message, but the wrath is brought on by those who choose to point fingers, who believe their salvation is better or more superior to someone else's, and believe that once they are born again they have no need to keep spiritually improving or to work for the social justice demanded by the Kingdom of God. *The wrath is coming* to those who refuse the peace of Christ, and that wrath is in fact something they have brought upon themselves.

Make no mistake about it, *this is how wrath of God works: we do it to ourselves*. The Good News of Jesus is that those left behind—those who work for peace and for justice—are remembered and gathered up by the winnowing shovel in the end.

We now return to John the Baptist's dirty joke. Who your parents, your grandparents, your spouses, and who your children are have no ultimate concern in the Kingdom of God that is built from the baptism of water and the Spirit. So of often baptisms become family events—next year we will likely baptize our new daughter and we'll have family from all over come for the event. That's all well and good, but John the Baptist is saying that the meaning of baptism is quite directly the opposite of this experience: that your family, and your financial concerns and community ties based on your family, may need to be deconstructed and broken down for the coming new order that the messiah brings. Claiming Abraham or anyone else as your ancestor, whether by blood or by spirit or anything else, does not ever make you right with God's graces.

And baptism should not fall into a lazy spiritual claim, as we always hear, about what defines us as Christians. So if being born again or being baptized gives you a sense of fulfillment that does not lead you to break the boundaries of religion and morality so commonly practiced in this world, then your baptism is not really a true baptism. If being born again makes you think that you're spiritually better than someone else, then you're not really born again, in fact, you are desperately in need of a second birth.

The bottom line here is that religious hypocrisy is everywhere in our society, and it is especially apparent to us the more and more Christmas is becoming secularized. It's not enough for us to complain about how we need to "keep Christ in Christmas" as we always hear. If we really are a baptized people, and if we really are a people born again through water and the Holy Spirit, the question is how are we working for justice, and the building of the Kingdom where the last are first and the first are last? What are we doing to castrate the powers and principalities of this world of backwardness and darkness, to lift up and prioritize the poor, and the widows, and those who make peace in this world? What are we doing to ensure that those few who fall through the cracks of the system are not left behind, so that we gather them up with shovels, rather than condemning them into the fire?

This past Friday, you, along with me, heard the horrific news of a school shooting in Newtown, Connecticut. Already fingers are politically pointing about the shootings. Should we expect more from the principalities and powers who rule this world? When we hear John the Baptist's condemnation of his followers, we easily impart his insult that "You brood of vipers" is always someone else, that someone else's mothers are snakes. If we want more gun control, it's the other side who is wrong. If we want less gun control, the other side are the bastard snakes.

We focus too much on the *vipers* in the phrase "You brood of vipers." We need to focus on the "you" and the "brood," the *brood* of vipers. Not all of us are snakes, exactly, but we all come from the same brood of vipers. We live in a culture apparently *too sensitive* to talk about the cause of children dying in their own school, but we are apparently *too insensitive* to the reality of violence that we are complacent with its continuance. We talk about people dying of violence but we call this conversation "political," and we say it's too controversial or partisan for preachers to talk about in pulpits.

The reality is that violence is a spiritual issue, and it is a matter of justice. Our children should not ever fear going to school. We should live in a world that strives to make safety an assumption and non-violence a *practice* of our faith.

I call upon the prophet Jeremiah:

> *Thus says the LORD:*
> *A voice is heard in Ramah,*
> *lamentation and bitter weeping.*
> *Rachel weeping for her children,*
> *because they are no more.*
> *Thus says the LORD:*
> *keep your voice from weeping*
> *and your eyes from tears,*
> *for there is reward for your work,*
> *says the LORD.* (Jeremiah 31:15–16, NRSV)

As we look around our world there is the rush leading to Christmas, one that is seemingly unstoppable next to the hush of the reality of this world bringing attention to itself. We are ready to celebrate the Christ child as a king, but we must also acknowledge that Christmas does not come for some. *The crucifixion of the world has instead continued and is continuing.* The screams of Rachel for her children are the songs of many for this Christmas season. We can have hope, but this Advent is now a time of lamentation.

*We are a brood of vipers.* Our brood caused this to happen. Our brood allows it to continue. Our brood only pays attention to it on occasion. Our brood largely does not care, even when the brood says that it does.

In many churches the Advent candles are named Hope, Peace, Joy, and Love. This morning we lit the joy candle for the third Sunday of Advent. This is presumptuous of us during this time of lamentation. Let us now seek out a joy that is truly a joy, a joy that is repentant, and a joy that seeks reconciliation in this world that is, for so many, a snake's nest.

## What to Expect When You're Expecting
(Advent 4)
*Luke 1:26–57*

In our Bible reading today we hear the famous exchange between the pregnant Elizabeth and the pregnant Mary, their children leaping in their bellies upon recognizing each other, and the famous song of Mary, often called the "Magnificat," a song that begins with the words, "My soul magnifies the Lord." Mary's answer to the angel Gabriel is also a famous line, she says, "Let it be with me according to your word."

It would be very easy to read this story, as many have in the past century, as a woman being subservient to a male God who has already impregnated her. We should be mindful that myths of virgins being raped by gods were not uncommon in other religions from the region at the time of Jesus, including the religion of the Greeks, who were the primary audience of the New Testament. I don't think it's wrong to think about this while thinking through this Biblical text, but one clue for considering this story among other pagan myths is in the Greek language with the word that is translated as "let it be with me according to your word." This word is "genoito" in Greek, which really has no English translation, is a rare kind of word in Greek that indicates a legal or contractual agreement. Mary's response is *genoito,* let it be with me according to your word. In other words, she might not have had a choice in the matter, but she agrees to the angel *as if she does have a choice.* She puts herself in control of the situation. This is all very different than other Greek myths of the time, and the Gospel writers were careful to make this distinction.

We should not obscure the shame involved with Mary's pregnancy also, as a pregnant teenager during this time in history. There have been some scholars who have suggested that the unmarried Jews during this time would get together before marriage, and if the girl became pregnant, it was seen as God blessing the marriage, so they would be married. This might seem a little farfetched until you consider that some Anabaptist sects actually do this as well today. Yet at the same time the Gospel of Luke goes far out of its way to call Mary a virgin and Luke says that she stayed with Elizabeth for three months but did not stay during the childbirth. I take this to mean that Mary was probably hiding her pregnancy as she was showing more, so she hid out at Elizabeth's home, and when John the Baptist was born, Mary went home, as an unmarried pregnant teenager would not have been allowed in the room or in the building during the birth of another child.

Even though Joseph is not a terribly important character in the way in which Luke tells the story, we should recall that he could have publicly shamed Mary and denied her marriage—which would have led her into a life of prostitution or perhaps even being stoned. If she would survive the stoning, the baby probably would not have survived. We need to take this into account when we consider Mary's words, *genoito,* "Let it be with me according to your word," that Mary is not only making a choice, but is making a contract with God, saying, I am faithful and I know, God, that you are faithful.

*  *  *

I have found that young women love to tell stories about how their children were born, and divulge the details of how things happened and in what order, what went wrong and what went right. Usually the story ends the same, the baby comes out and the husband gets sick at the sight, but the rest of the stories are different. I have come to determine that birthing stories always operate with their own logic. The story of each birth is different and happens differently for very different reasons.

As I have heard more and more stories about women who have lost pregnancies, I have similarly come to the conclusion that the loss of children also operates with its own logic—there is really no sense to be made of miscarriage rather than that it happened. Clearly, for some women there may be conditions that lead to a terminal pregnancy, but in terms of making sense of it, there is no making sense.

We are called as Christians to accept Christ into our hearts as Mary accepted Christ into her womb. We all have our own reasons and stories of our spiritual births, and in this church we don't believe that our acceptance of Christ has to be exactly the same or mean the same things—often there is no logic to how or why we are Christians, but what is important is that we have Christ in our hearts, and *then we do something* with that Christ in our hearts.

For many of us, and I believe this is true of many of us in this church, we were born Christian, baptized Christian, confirmed Christian, married Christian, and we expect to have a Christian burial.

But today we hear this story of Mary, knowing all of the potential risks and heartache that may lie involved with accepting a baby, reply to the angel with the Greek word *genoito,* "let it be with me according to your word," and we know that we just can't let Christ *be* in our hearts, but we must let Christ *become* part of our bodies and our thinking; we must let Christ leap in our bellies when we encounter others with Christ in them; we must make ourselves to have a good home for Christ in our bodies; we must understand that having Christ in our hearts grafts us onto a history that goes far beyond our parents and our church but back to the beginning of human history, and that God works with those often deemed unworthy by everyone else; we must have joy with the birth pangs of the Kingdom of Christ that is giving birth to a New Creation all around us; and we must make Christ known to each other when we occasionally stumble or lose Christ in our hearts.

## Palm Sunday in December
(The Nativity & Christmas Eve)
*Luke 2:1–7*

A reading from the book of Islam, the Qur'an, Sura 19:

*Mention in the scripture Mary. She isolated herself from her family, into an eastern location. While a barrier separated her from them, we sent to her our Spirit. He went to her in the form of a human being.*

*Mary said, "I seek refuge in the Most Gracious, that you may be righteous."*

*He said, "I am the messenger of your Lord, to grant you a pure son."*

*She said, "How can I have a son, when no man has touched me, I have never been unchaste."*

*He said, "Thus said your Lord, 'It is easy for Me. We will render him a sign for the people, and mercy from us. This is a predestined matter.'*

*When she bore him, she isolated herself to a faraway place. The birth process came to her by the trunk of a palm tree. She said, "I am so ashamed; I wish I were dead before this happened, and completely forgotten."*

*The infant [Jesus] called her from beneath her, saying, "Do not grieve. Your Lord has provided you with a stream. If you shake the trunk of this palm tree, it will drop ripe dates for you. Eat and drink, and be happy. When you see anyone, say, 'I have made a vow of silence; I am not talking today to anyone.'"*

*She came to her family, carrying him. They said, "O Mary, you have committed something that is totally unexpected. O descendent of Aaron, your father was not a bad man, nor was your mother unchaste."*

*She pointed to him [Jesus]. They said, "How can we talk with an infant in the crib?"*

*The infant spoke and said, "I am a servant of Allah. He has*

> *given me the scripture, and has appointed me a prophet. He made me blessed wherever I go, and enjoined me to observe the salat and the zakat for as long as I live. I am to honor my mother; He did not make me a disobedient rebel. And peace be upon me the day I was born, the day I die, and the day I get resurrected."*
>
> *That was Jesus, the son of Mary, and this is the truth of this matter, about which they continue to doubt. It does not befit Allah that He begets a son, be He glorified. To have anything done, he simply says to it, "Be," and it is. He also proclaimed, "Allah is my Lord and your Lord; you shall worship Him alone. This is the right path."*[1]

One thing that really struck me the first time I read the Qur'an is how much of the Christian Bible is present in the Qur'an, and how much reverence Muslims have for Jesus as a historical figure and prophet. Muslims don't believe that Jesus was God, and they don't really believe that Jesus died in a crucifixion which led to a resurrection, but Muslims do believe in the virgin birth of Jesus, and while they don't believe that Jesus rose from the dead, Muslims believe in the raising of the dead on the Day of Judgment. This really struck me because, while I have a deep faith in the resurrection of Jesus on the first Easter, the Virgin Birth story is one that I have always struggled with and I have learned to simply accept the story as a story, a story with deep meaning, but not one that I am going to get my faith hung-up over.

Whenever I read the Qur'an, I am genuinely struck again by how much more there is of Mary in the Islamic holy book—in fact, there is more about Mary than just about anyone else from the Christian story in the Qur'an. Muslims believe in her perpetual virginity—the belief that Catholics have that Mary remained a virgin throughout her life—and Muslims elevate her status to a higher position than Protestants, her station as the mother of Jesus seems very Catholic to me, and perhaps even very, very Christian. Mary is the only woman who is actually mentioned by name in the whole book of the Qur'an, and there is more content devoted to her in the Qur'an than in the Bible.

What also strikes me are the differences between the birth narrative of Jesus in the New Testament and the Qur'an. As we know, in the Christian version of the story, or at least in one of the Christian versions of the story, Mary and Joseph travel together, and Joseph does not shun Mary for being a single mother, and Mary accompanies Joseph to Bethlehem, where they find no vacancy in any of the inns. Because of the fact she is pregnant, she is given a barn to deliver Jesus into the world.

But in the Muslim version of the story, Mary travels alone, Joseph is not with her, and she gives birth to Jesus under a single palm tree. As the story goes, Mary, traveling in the desert, knew that the time was now to give birth to the baby Jesus. Near a palm tree, she grasped onto the tree, and Jesus began to speak words of comfort to her from within her womb, and as a result Mary vowed not to speak to any man on the day of Jesus' birth, which she held true, as she only had a palm tree as a midwife for the delivery of Jesus.[2]

I am quite taken by the two different portrayals of Jesus' birth: one, Mary gives birth to Jesus surrounded by her new husband and barn animals. In fact, in most of our nativity scenes around the church, and in our homes, we invite the whole cast into Jesus' birth scene: shepherds, wise men, and stars—and we like to portray the barn as not being enclosed, as if Jesus' delivery was a kind of public event, which might explain why there was such a crowd gathering!

On the other hand, in the Muslim story we have Mary, alone, with only the comfort of a random tree, and the movements of the interiors of her womb to comfort her. The Qur'an goes out of its way to teach that Mary had no companions, no male companions, and not even a barn in which to give birth. She had not even reached her destination as she gave birth in the middle of the desert. The only gifts she received from the world, the Qur'an says, is that the palm tree provided dates for her to eat to give her sustenance after giving birth to Jesus.

What strikes me about these images are the locations of Christmas that we find ourselves at different times in our lives, and the contradictory ways that we locate ourselves with others around the holidays. We come to church and worship with others—and the church is a little more full during Advent and Christmas than other times of the year. We may have family gatherings before or after Christmas, or even on Christmas Eve and Christmas day. We may attend Christmas parties or carol with friends, or have carolers interrupt our evening with singing in the neighborhood. We may even find Christmas cards in our mailboxes, and receive and give gifts.

But we also contrast this community celebration with the loneliness that many of us experience during the Christmas season. Many of us go from being overwhelmed to being alone quite suddenly, and the sudden transition from being around lots of friends and family to being in an empty home seems a bit more jaunting during the holidays. I had years in graduate school where I had a tradition of making myself a frozen pizza for Christmas every year and watching *Star Wars* by myself. But even if we are surrounded by our friends and families, we recognize the joy of new faces that gather around our tables and the absences of those who are no longer with us during the holidays for any number of reasons. The presence of their absence sometimes stings more harshly during these cold and bitter days of the holidays.

We can relate to Mary during the holidays in both stories—Mary surrounded, and Mary alone. But in both cases the comfort given to Mary is the delivery of the Christ child, a delivery of God into the world for the delivery of God's people, that is, all of humanity, all of us, to be liberated from the wages of oppression and death. That even in loneliness in the desert, God provided for Mary with the fruit of the palm tree, and that the palm tree is part of God's plan: We should remember that, in this version of the story, the trunk of the palm tree helped deliver Jesus, the fruit of the tree sustained Mary, and later, on Palm Sunday, the branches of the palm tree welcome Jesus into the city of Jerusalem as a King, to overthrow the hypocrites in the mainstream of society, only to be betrayed and killed a few days later.

The Jesus story might be the story of the Palm tree—that God provides and sustains his plan for us in ways that are unexpected, unplanned, interrupting, ironic, and sometimes not with the most pleasant events. But through unpleasantness and loneliness and grieving, we find assurance of being part of God's love and protection and being part of God's plan.

In the Christian version of the story, Mary came into town with her husband, soon to become teenage parents, on the run from the law, to find inns with "No Vacancy" signs. We stand today in these last days of Advent, too, with "No Vacancy" signs hanging over our hearts. We don't have enough money, we don't have enough time, we don't have room in our inns for more presence or interruptions of the Holy in our lives. We are too busy, our schedules and calendars say "no vacancy" to those in our families and community who need our vacancies, and, as such, no vacancy for the Christ who is waiting to be delivered. Not even having a barn, very often we leave Mary out in the desert to only be comforted by the shade of a palm tree, even while we ourselves spiritually have only the shade of a palm tree to offer.

Instead, we should choose neither of these stories as our Christmas story, but subvert both of them, and authentically invite the Christ child to truly occupy our homes, our barns, our desks, our offices, our cars, our family and neighborly relationships, and most importantly, our church. The world did not truly accept Jesus as God in 2,000 years ago, and now is as good as time as any to understand that the Christmas story is not about the details of history but instead is the lure of opening the doors of our hearts and the doors of ourselves, to expose ourselves to one another and to open a window for the Spirit to blow in and a new rose to be planted in the bleak midwinter. It is now time to open our hearts to Jesus, a Jesus whose power transforms us from the inside out, the same Christ who leaped and spoke from the womb of Mary now resurrects and transfigures our hearts and spirits.

I know that it is still Advent and not yet Christmas. But my Good News message is for us to prepare the way of the Lord for this Christmas to be one that more authentically bears Christ in new ways we may have though unimaginable before—whether we find ourselves jolted by the overwhelming nature of the season or the blueness and loneliness of the season, Christ comes to us in both abundance and in solitude. We often don't get to choose the context and situations in which we find ourselves in the holidays, but we do get to choose whether the Christ-child comes as a story which brings us sadness and mourning over the holidays, or choose the Christ child who brings us a deep joy and comfort that pierces through our tough times. The choice, and this community challenge to bear it for others, is now upon us for each other.

## Come, Lord Jesus[1]
(The Feast of St. John)
*Exodus 20:15–21; 1 John 1:1–2:1a*

Christmas has arrived; we now proceed through the lesser days of Christmas, where the excitement of the season has waned, the excitement and wonder has diminished in the secular world, yet we continue the season of Christmastide on this feast of St. John.

In 1 John 1 we hear that "[i]f we say we have fellowship in [God] while we are walking in darkness, we lie and do not do what is true," and "[i]f we say we have no sin, we deceive ourselves, and the truth is not in us." Finally, a famous line of scripture: "God is light and in him there is no darkness at all."

The idea of "light" is an enormously important spiritual concept, but it has different meanings, and we have to relate to the Biblical author, who obviously wrote these words down before electricity has made light something we often take for granted. Within the context of the whole book of 1 John, the primary meaning of light has to do with moral purity, that God does not sin and God is not tainted by sin. We also think of light in an obvious way, that light shines out of darkness.

This is why the lighting of candles is so memorable and beautiful on Christmas Eve, singing "Silent Night." As the pastor, when I watch it from the pulpit, the congregation becomes an ocean of lights glimmering out of darkness. Furthermore, at least for me, the experience is also theologically meaningful, that we testify to the light by lighting our own little lights.

But allow me to get a little philosophical. If all we know is light, we would need darkness to know the light. Similarly, if all we know is darkness, we would need light to know that we live in darkness.

In the book of Exodus, the beginning of God's revelation in the form of law, perhaps the most important moment of God's word for the Hebrews is the Ten Commandments. Interestingly, God reveals the Ten Commandments from a thick cloud of darkness, according to the scriptures.

So it would seem that to speak in absolutes—God is darkness, or God is light—is a bit of an overstatement, because if God is anything, God, or our conception of God, must embody a *coincidence of opposites:* binaries which occur as nonpolar binaries; dialectically defining oneself through and by the other. Recall that God speaks from the darkness; God reveals through the light. If light shines out of the darkness, can the darkness be entirely understood to be negative? God sweeps over the darkness of the deep at the moment of creation.[2] God reveals power over the political powers and foreign religious systems by casting darkness over Egypt.[3] Just as Moses encounters God through the thick cloud of darkness, so also does King Solomon praise God by recalling the darkness of God.[4] The crucifixion of Jesus is also cast in darkness; and tradition teaches that Jesus descends into the darkness of Hell to liberate those who are enslaved in the darkness.[5]

This is all to say, darkness is a double-edged sword. Often the bad things that happen in the presence of, or symbolized by, darkness are from a different perspective, good. Why else do we call the day that we commemorate the darkness of Jesus' death on the cross "Good Friday?"

\* \* \*

Ours is a dark age. The past months and the news of the past months seem almost overwhelmingly bad. Even after the expectancy of the season of Advent, and after the arrival of the Christ child in Bethlehem, we still lay in wait, too passively, in today's advent, today's waiting, for Christ. It would seem that the only prayer that we have left is "Come, Lord Jesus."

*Come, Lord Jesus.*

In this past year our church has grown, but we have also lost some beloved members who have died. Their presence is felt perhaps the strongest during the holiday season. When we face such loss, and peer into the darkness of our own mortality, the only prayer that we have left is "Come, Lord Jesus."

*Come, Lord Jesus.*

The recent revelation that our government has been engaging in torture of its prisoners to a point of escalation beyond what many of us thought was unfathomable by our own people, has reminded us again that to place our hope into systems of power on this earth is a grave mistake when Jesus is our only hope of the world. And yet while we still place hope in dumb idols, we pray, "Come, Lord Jesus."

*Come, Lord Jesus.*

So many of our families are in conflict during this holiday season, so many people are feeling hurt by divisions and discrimination by faith communities during these holy days. Where we have contributed to the broken body, we pray, "Come, Lord Jesus."

*Come, Lord Jesus.*

For the emphasis of world events on religious tyranny, and religious hatred, in the emerging Islamic Caliphate in the Middle East, and among the poorest of Africa, and the persecution of Palestine, we often have no genuine words to say or to pray but "Come, Lord Jesus."

*Come, Lord Jesus.*

For the racism that exists everywhere around us, and defines so much of our culture, and our inability to recognize it and speak loudly and clearly out of the silence with a prophet's tongue, striving for justice, we pray: "Come, Lord Jesus."

*Come, Lord Jesus.*

\* \* \*

A thick cloud surrounds our experiences. When we descend deeper into the darkness of God, where darkness envelops darkness, where the luminosity of darkness has nothing but potential for light, it is there where the light, however small, becomes more meaningful, more hopeful, more salvific, more joyous.

Through this darkness God speaks, and God incarnates as a fragile child in the womb of Mary. That which is pure and morally without blemish enters the world into a tenuous place, the insides of an unmarried teenage girl: a place where the princes and powers of this world still to this day spend much effort and rhetoric to legislate and control. Just as God speaks over the waters of creation, God speaks new life, *Godself*, into a place that the people of that time did not biologically understand, and was—and is—a source of fear, a source of darkness to men. God enters this world, from being nestled in dark waters.

When the waters break, out of the darkness of the womb, God arrives into the world just as every one of us has. Like all babies, the shock from traveling from darkness to light overwhelms the senses, and with the light comes coldness, shivering, and a desire to return to the safety of darkness. But just like all of us, the baby Jesus acclimated to the light.

The world of light into which Jesus arrives was a world in the darkness of night. A world where two teenage parents were on the run from the law as undocumented refugees hiding from the Empire; a world where the same political powers sought to destroy any remnant of true light in the darkness by killing scores of children. The working poor, the shepherds, and displaced foreign intellectuals, the wise men from the east, followed the small light shining out of darkness to find the enfleshed baby God.

It is said that Christmas is a time of wonder. Our purest Christmas hymns and carols evoke a sense of wonder—"I Wonder as I Wander"; "Let All Mortal Flesh Keep Silence"; "Lo, How a Rose E'er Blooming"; "In the Bleak Midwinter"—when we listen to Christmas and holiday songs on the radio the *mystery* of Christmas is precisely what is absent from today's music and our experiences. Similarly, so much of our holiday experiences are obsessively planned and very carefully executed: we know where we will be and what we will probably eat, and who we will be with and who we will not be with during this holiday season. Children have prepared their lists for Santa Claus since Halloween. In the marketplace, Christmas has become a mockery of itself, while zealots rage on about a war on Christmas that isn't really happening, arguing that Christmas should be something it entirely is not. We all know this.

We all *know* this, but it is our knowing, our knowledge, our illusion of knowledge defeats us. *We know too much about Christmas.* The unknowing, or true wonderment, of Christmas is something for which we have yet to fully strive: the safety of what we know about Christmas. Christmas is not at all predictable: it is an interruption, a movement between *coincidences of opposites*: from darkness comes forth light. From the distance of God in heaven to the nearness of our space, our time, our flesh, our death. When we pray, "Come, Lord Jesus"—*Come, Lord Jesus*—we petition for an inbreaking of surprise, a disconnect from what was previously *too connected*, the shattering of something desperately in need of shattering, yet this light is hindered, and apprehended, and resisted by a world and its powers so enshrouded by *darkness pretending to be light*.

Perhaps what we are called to do is to subvert the light, or lightness, of Christmas with the darkness of Christmas, so that the luminosity of the holy may shine through. That we might carry ourselves with expectancy and expectation as Mary, and break the silence of Zechariah, and prophesy to the stars to fall to this earth as did Isaiah: seeking for God to arrive again, through us, in this present moment. An arrival of God so calamitous and scandalous that the powers and kings shall shiver, the tables of the holiday marketplaces shall be overthrown, and a world where equality and the justice of God finally reign.

This was the vision of this little baby boy, this God, being born in a barn, surrounded by the stench of animals, their feed, their droppings: that the last will be first and the first will be last. If God can be born out of darkness, can we ourselves vision God birthing into the world through us?

Come, Lord Jesus.
*Come, Lord Jesus.*
Come, Lord Jesus.
*Come, Lord Jesus.*
Come, Lord Jesus.
*Come, Lord Jesus.*

## Crib Notes from Bethlehem[1]
(Holy Name of Jesus)
*Galatians 4:4–7*

St. Paul writes that "when the fullness of time had come, God sent his Son, born of a woman, born under the law, in order to redeem those who were under the law, so that we might receive adoption as children," continuing, and "because you are children, God has sent the Spirit of his Son into our hearts, crying, 'Abba! Father'!" Therefore, we are no longer a slave, but a child, and if a child then also an heir, through God."

This passage from scripture from St. Paul in Galatians 4 is probably everything we need to theologically know about Christmas in just a few sentences, that God submits to the logic of sacrifice, to be sacrificed on the cross by entering human form, and submitting to the law or logic of humanity. And as a result, we are all children of the same divine Parent: no longer slaves to the ways of the world but heirs to inherit the Kingdom of God by building the Kingdom of God for ourselves and for future generations.

But is this really how it all works? Have we ever realized the brotherhood and sisterhood of humanity in our time? Have we ever found a way to subvert the system of violence and crucifixion that this world has known? I believe that many of our nations and much of humanity may believe that we have achieved this first step of bringing peace on earth and goodwill to humankind, but we know we have really cheated the full sense of what it means to acknowledge that God is born in a manger.

There is something special about the Christmas carol "Away in a Manger," aside from how theologically problematic, or even Docetist, as a heresy, the words are: "no crying he makes." As a lullaby that we sing to children, we sometimes miss out that when we sing the song "Away in a Manger" to children, we are, in essence, ordaining children to lead us as children to become closer to God.

What would this world be like if we not only recognized the Christhood and the Godhood present in the new flesh of babies and children, and honor the sacredness of this humanity God has come to save? We know that with the number of children living in poverty and in hunger in our country and everywhere in the world, we have not only turned our backs upon the world but we have turned our backs upon God-made-flesh. Or perhaps stated more accurately, it would seem that the behavior of this world has in fact *stolen* the divinity and sacredness of cribs of unsuspecting children throughout the world.

A first step for us to move forward is to recognize that we, too, have had our Christhood stolen from the crib, as well, that we too are victims of this world as we participate in the victimization of the world. And recognizing that the God who is made known to us in newborn flesh is with us, and in us, living and breathing, and perishing with us.

If the Christ-child has been abducted from our lives, it's time to return him into our hearts, and into our spirits. If we have cheated in responding to the Good News of Christmas, it is now time to rectify our commitment to the Kingdom of God, whose birth pangs are ringing loudly around us in Christmas bells, and festive lights, and carols, and in the anticipation of the Christhood delivered to us as a child being born on this dark and cold night.

## Coyote Gospel
(Baptism of the Lord / Epiphany 1)
*Isaiah 43:1–7, Acts 8:14–17*

In Acts 8, we hear the short story of Peter and John preaching in Samaria. With many new conversions to the new Christian faith, a movement not yet a distinctly separate religion from Judaism, Peter and John prayed that they might "receive" the Holy Spirit, and then when they laid their hands upon the new converts, the scripture says, they "received" the Holy Spirit.

I ask: What does it mean to "receive" the Holy Spirit? Usually this passage of scripture is interpreted to mean that some kind of magical event of the Holy Spirit occurs, and these new followers are filled with the Holy Spirit. I think this is some of what the story is implying here, but there are two meanings of the word "receive." First is to be a recipient, as if you "receive" a gift; the second meaning is to be hospitable to something, so as to "receive" guests.

In the first sense of the word "receive," the new converts were given the Holy Spirit simply through prayer and the laying of hands. It is for this reason the laying of hands is considered such an important part of Christian ritual that the minister touches the bread and wine while praying for the Holy Spirit to come upon the elements in communion, or when we have confirmations, or baptisms, we lay hands. When I officiate a wedding, the very last blessing includes an act where I put my hands upon the joined hands of the bride and groom, as a means of filling this new union with the Holy Spirit. So, in the first sense of "receive," the Holy Spirit is given as a gift to persons through the laying of hands.

To return to the scripture, if we take the receiving as the Holy Spirit as the second meaning of the word "receive," as in *receiving* a guest, it means something a little different when we're talking about people receiving the Holy Spirit: instead of having already acquired the Holy Spirit, of commanding the Holy Spirit, they are instead *welcoming* the

Holy Spirit to come upon them. They are 'preparing room' for the Spirit in their hearts.

Often we meet Christians who believe that they have received the Holy Spirit, and this gives them some authority over others. This is the first meaning of "receive." I'm much more interested in people who receive the Holy Spirit in the second way of defining the word: I am much more attracted to people of faith who are humble, and open to the Spirit, rather than trumpeting that we already have the Spirit. It is the difference between commanding others to conform to me verses being open to being changed radically from the inside out.

If we think of the Holy Spirit as something we have or don't have, or that receiving the Spirit makes someone better than others, it places the rest of us in a kind of Catch-22: we are always then striving for God, but we just never get there. It reminds me of the cartoons with Wile E. Coyote and the Road Runner: the coyote just never seems to catch the Road Runner, and the more he tries the more desperate he becomes. And the more he tries the more obstacles get in the way.

What would happen if Wile E. Coyote ever caught the Road Runner? There's actually a YouTube video on the internet that parodies the Road Runner cartoons, beginning with the coyote catching the road runner, kind of by accident, and he eats him. And then he asks: Now what? What do I do with my life now?

The coyote takes a job and is unfulfilled and gets depressed. He gets fired from his job, and contemplates suicide. Then he has a religious epiphany and finds Jesus.[1] The coyote, in his moment of despair, receives the Holy Spirit and wants to tell everyone about it. He finally found certainty and clarity about his life.

The coyote receives the Holy Spirit in the first sense of the word: *he has found certainty*. Since he caught the elusive Road Runner, God is the next elusive *thing* to be caught. We all know people who are authority figures in one profession, but then believe they found Jesus and go into churches and act as if they are above reproach: "Because I was highly successful in business, or in the military, I have proven that I have caught something elusive, and here's what I can tell you about Jesus, because I caught him, too!" We do this with our politicians, too, especially when people start talking about Donald Trump for President: He knows how to make money off of bankruptcy, so he'd be perfect as the leader of the free world, right? We know the type, and we participate with this process in our own culture: with the Road Runner gone, we substitute the bird for something else equally elusive. Often that *thing* is God; and in doing so, we tear down the mystery and transcendence and wonder of God to be a *thing,* a dumb idol which may be *grasped.* We, in turn, *objectify* God, or render this *thing, God,* as an *object.*

But what if the coyote *received* the Holy Spirit in a different way, where he *welcomed* the Holy Spirit, rather than act as if he has chased and grasped the God? Now, I doubt that Wile E. Coyote could do such a thing, because it is the nature of his character to *chase things.* If he could do this, would the coyote be happier if he just stopped chasing the Road Runner years ago and welcomed him into his life as something other than a sacrifice for his own gratification—recognizing that the Road Runner, if caught, would only make one good meal.

While thinking about the adventures of Wile E. Coyote and the Road Runner this past week, I also remembered in elementary school watching a cartoon about the way that American democracy works that used these cartoon characters. The one thing I remembered from that film—and it took me a little while, but I found it on the internet this week—is that the narrator says that the reason why the U.S. Constitution is so great is because it protects the freedom of the individual to succeed, and, the narrator adds, "and sometimes, to fail," as the coyote goes off of a cliff trying to catch the Road Runner. The cliff, of course, is Mount Rushmore.[2]

This image has always stuck with me as an open admission that the way our society works is that it protects success as it protects, ensures, and guarantees failure, at least for someone. Someone will succeed and with someone's success there will always be someone who fails. The irony is that Wile E. Coyote is a prime example of how we are taught we succeed in America: Keep trying, keep practicing, keep being persistent. But the Coyote is always a failure because the system necessitates failure. We as the audience enjoy watching the coyote fail as a scapegoat. He makes us feel better that someone else fails. But yet, we, like the coyote, never seem to get whatever it is we are running after.

My point is that in life we are always searching for that *thing* we are always going after, we might say that it is "God" or wisdom that we are searching for something spiritual, but when it comes down to it most of what we do is for our own survival and sustainability. Very often when we do things for our spiritual lives it is about ensuring a place in the pearly-gated community known as "heaven." We never seem to have enough money, and we can never seem to get enough of it. We confuse not having enough money for all of the things that we could possibly want to be poor or underprivileged. We see the things others have, and we construct ourselves to be rivals for the things we don't have. This is the history of the world from the beginning, every war can be explained though this very basic truth, from Cain and Abel to the modern day.

But here in the book of Acts, the disciples' ministry *opens the window of the Holy Spirit,* and the Apostles and the early church went out from there to preach about their faith, and talk to their friends and family about their faith, and to witness, and in some cases die for the sake of their faith. There is no rivalry. Here, in this early church, there is no constant chase or perpetual conflict. The new society that is emerging is totally New. Family rivalries are no more. All of these things that are part of the old world now become past tense, and there is only the new world that is the New Creation Now Occurring. There are no individuals in the body of Christ on this day, but they are the *living Christ* and they become God for the world on this day.

The new converts did not claim to be better than the other. They were simply open to receive—the second use of the word *receive*—open to the reception of the Holy Spirit. And we are to do likewise. Our homes and our church have become stuffy. We have relied too heavily upon the warmth of ourselves, and the heat of our conflicts, and the money of dead people to make the air heavy and stagnant. It is now time for us to crack open a window for the Holy Spirit. Maybe the stained glass needs to be opened up. One of the pervasive teachings of the Bible on the Holy Spirit and one of the most important historic doctrines of our United Church of Christ faith heritage is that the Holy Spirit blows where it chooses, but will only enter if we are *ready to receive* and welcome the Holy Spirit as an interrupting and expected guest. If we think we have no need to receive the Spirit, we just keep doing what we always do. We then acknowledge that conflict and stagnancy is what we want. We are just fine to, as the book of Ecclesiastes proclaims, "chase after the wind."

Are we prepared for a Holy Spirit interruption which shatters the stained glass? We need the earthquake of the resurrection to render the temple curtain torn. This is the age of the Holy Spirit, not the age of a church boldly prepared for the 1950s. It's now our choice whether we take this step into uncertainty or *cling* to the certainties of the past. It might feel like walking the plank. But if that is what it is, we walk off of the cliff with faith and confidence that we will be guided through the darkness with and through the Holy Spirit.

Because in the end, that's all we have as a church: The Holy Spirit.

## When Atheists Come for Pizza
(Epiphany 5)
*Luke 5:1–11*

*Several years ago, an atheist advocacy group held a meeting at a local pizza shop, which led to some local Christians protesting the pizza shop and harassing customers who continued to patronize the shop. This led to an ongoing debate about discrimination against atheists: the Christians' behavior in turn validated the necessity for atheists to organize, even if covertly. The pizza shop went out of business a few years later.*

The fishermen are done for the day and the fishing hasn't been good. Jesus tells the men to throw the nets into the waters one last time, and they got so many fish that the boat almost toppled over. Simon immediately recognizes what has happened as a miracle, and asks Jesus to leave, because he is not worthy to be in his presence, but Jesus tells him that he has nothing to be afraid of in his presence and famously says, "you will now be fishers of men."

If you've been following some of the local news, you know that roughly three weeks ago a group of atheists from Harrisburg met in a local pizzeria here in Lebanon. I don't think the local newspaper mentioned which pizza shop it was, but the local talk radio station did, and I don't remember which pizza shop it was. Regardless, when they came to meet in the pizza shop, they were greeted with a few protesters who took photos of everyone going in for pizza that evening and refused to speak to the atheists.[1]

Concurrently, while waiting for someone from the church to come out of surgery a couple weeks ago, I overheard some other people in the waiting room talking about the atheists who came for pizza. They spoke that they were ashamed that a group of atheists came to town, and that they won't buy pizza from the shop anymore, but then they went into a long rant about how the pizza shop owners were surely going to Hell for allowing the atheists to eat there. It's important to remember that when we see the extreme religious voices in our community that might sound ridiculous, that they're often saying what people are thinking, or what people are thinking but are afraid to say.

The reality of our situation today is that more and more people are considering themselves atheists. You surely have atheists in your family, and you surely have atheists in your workplace. They're all around us.

Today is not the place to evaluate the positions of atheists beyond this: I believe that the new rise and prevalence of atheism in our culture is saying something about the stagnance and flaccidity of Christianity, especially when Christianity postures itself as an authoritarian, patriarchal, and absolute faith that promises the lie of absolute certainty about God and absolute certainty about the nature of the universe.

This is to say that atheism is a call to the church that we have taken for granted what Christianity is and is not and forget just how socially radical Christianity could or should be, that the Christianity rejected by atheists is the religion of the foolish who protest pizza shops in the name of Jesus, who believe that welcoming atheists into a restaurant will condemn you to Hell. We can often say that those who protest pizza shops or dead soldiers' funerals is not really Christianity, but we're lying to ourselves if we don't acknowledge that deep down, many Christians, and many of us, feel the same way. We just don't have the guts to proclaim it out loud.

The radicalism of the Gospel is illustrated in today's story from the Bible. If you can imagine Jesus interrupting these men at work on the docks—I imagine rough, dirty men, hungry from a long day, swearing because they worked for nothing and have nothing to take home to their families. They have had days like this, and it's often expected to have bad days, but they're discouraged and ready to go home.

But Jesus interrupts the scene by coming in and telling them where to fish. They surely did what he said just as a joke, but were overwhelmed with how many fish they took out of the lake.

Something to think through is the symbolic meaning of the harvesting all of the fish. First of all, it was a miracle that it all happened, but we should remember that there was no refrigeration back then and also that Lake Gennessaret was a body of water with a fairly fragile ecosystem, and we know that fishermen knew the basics of these things during this time—in other words, taking out such a quantity of fish surly presented a challenge that long-term, they would make less money off of the fish and there would be less fish to catch, and short-term, they had to get rid of all of this fish that they had just caught all night long.

What is so interesting to me here is that with this interruption of business as usual on the fishing dock, Simon asks Jesus to leave because he is not worthy and Jesus commands Simon to leave with him. It would seem that denying Jesus lends us greater reason to leave, and when Simon leaves, he is not only leaving his family and his business, but the men who fished with him and who had his back while he was out on the water. He was leaving everything behind, but perhaps most importantly, he was leaving behind the very thing that stood between following Jesus and not following Jesus, namely, a disbelief that Jesus would want someone like him to follow.

The Good News for us today is not to condemn the atheist for coming for pizza, but rather to invite and witness that the reason why we're Christian isn't because we're right about the world or that our understanding of science or politics is superior, but because trusting in God and living in a Christ-bearing manner gives us joy and leads us to serve others in ways that reflect the grace God pours out for us.

Instead of throwing the Bible at the atheist we should *invite* the atheist to read the Bible with us and to learn from them, in the hopes that they understand that reading the Bible isn't about finding an answer key to all of life's big questions, but more about choosing to live as a people connected to the greatest story ever told.

Instead of hassling the pizza shop owners, we should sit down and eat with the atheist, even if it's pizza, to demonstrate the way that we pray when we eat gives reverence not only for the God whom we believe to be supreme, but as good stewards of the gifts of food and water that give us sustenance. Besides, we have lots of fish left over from the Sea of Galilee to put on the pizza as anchovies.

So go and buy your closest atheist a slice of pizza and don't just tell him or her the Good News, but show them how the love of God reflects a love for them, too, that as a people struggling to reconcile with what is true and false and right and wrong in the world, that we all come as equal sinners to the altar of Christ. And like Simon Peter, the less worthy we appear, the more likely it is that Jesus calls us to go and make a radical change to follow him.

The Seasons of Lent and Eastertide

## Why I Should Be Pope
(Lent 1)
*(Genesis 3:1–13) Romans 10:8b-13, Luke 4:1–13*

*This sermon was preached immediately following the resignation of Pope Benedict XVI and before the ascension of Pope Francis I, in late winter, 2013.*

In our scripture reading, Jesus heads out into the wilderness, and there he is tempted by the devil, who challenges him to perform a magic trick of turning a rock into bread. When Jesus refuses, the devil, the scripture says, "led him up" (it doesn't say, *up where,* but the devil *leads him up,* I assume to a high point on a mountain, or high in the sky) and offers Jesus all of the kingdoms of the world, if he were to simply worship the devil, and Jesus again refuses.

Then the devil tempts Jesus again, taking him to the pinnacle of the temple and again demands a miracle, that he throw himself from the pinnacle and command the angels to save him from death. The devil famously quotes scripture here, and after Jesus resists the temptations of the devil, the devil departs from him until a more "opportune time."

Among the things interesting about this story is that there is an assumption that the devil owns all of the kingdoms, and Jesus does not say to the devil, "these are not your kingdoms to give." There is no indication that the devil is lying to Jesus. And it is not just that *some* of the kingdoms are his to give, or only those within immediate view, the Bible instructs that it is *"all* of the kingdoms" that belong to the devil. None of the kingdoms or governments escape control of the devil, *none of them are holy.*

So from this implied condemnation of all governments, Jesus is taken to the highest point of the temple. The pinnacle of the temple would have been a wing-shaped small structure at the highest point on the southeastern corner of the Second Temple that would have looked about

350 feet down toward the Valley of Kidron. It's worth noting that our Lenten journey begins this Sunday with Jesus being tempted at the point of the temple looking down upon the same area where he entered Jerusalem on a donkey on Palm Sunday, and later that final week would cross the valley from the place of his last meal to the Garden of Gethsemane. Those who first heard this Gospel read to them would have known the geography of the area and made these connections of the beginning point of Jesus' temptation to the end of his journey into human death.

But those also familiar with the geography of the area would know that directly down from where the pinnacle of the temple was, in this Valley of Kidron, is an interesting, ancient structure known today as the Tomb of Absalom. This structure has traditionally been believed to be the resting place of the body of King David's rebellious son, Absalom, but scholars have more recently debunked that it is not actually Absalom's tomb, and they believe that the structure was built at about the time of Jesus' life or the writing of the Gospel of Luke.

Scholars today are of two minds what this structure is that Jesus would have looked down, from here the devil suggested the angels save him. The first is that the tomb is not at all a tomb but is a monument for a system of burial caves nearby. The other theory is that at some point the structure became known to be the burial site of the father of John the Baptist, Zechariah, who is believed to have been killed by being sawed in half. And related to this is that nearby to this structure is another ancient structure called the Tomb of Zechariah, which is referring to another Zechariah, who was the last victim of murder in the Hebrew Scriptures, whom Jesus references directly in the Gospel of Matthew.[1]

That is, when the devil takes Jesus "up" to see all of the kingdoms, he offered what they saw together to him, and then they went on top of the temple, specifically to the highest point that looked down upon a valley where, directly below, is a system of caves for burying the dead, a monument that may be a reminder of the harsh death of both John the Baptist and his father, and the nearby tomb of the last violent murder of the Old Testament.

*What does the devil ask him to do, upon seeing this view?* Throw yourself into this valley of death, and let the angels save you! If you're a God, you don't have to die, you can command the angelic powers to deliver you from death! If you know Greek literature, the tragedy of death is reserved for human beings, and not to Gods. The Good News of Jesus is precisely that Jesus, as God, does not shun human death, and he does not save himself from it, but that the perishing and death of God on the cross is the ultimate act of sacrifice of God for humanity. The devil tries to trick God into acting like other gods. Jesus' divinity for us is demonstrated through a denial of this characteristic or attribute that makes gods godly, namely, their inability to die a human death.

\* \* \*

Similar to my statement earlier that the Gospel of Luke makes the automatic assumption that the kingdoms of the world are the devil's to dispense, so also is it important to me to read this story with the implication that the devil is hanging out and has some control over Jesus at the highest point of the temple. The temple was understood as the center of the universe to the Jews, and the statement being made here is that if the temple were running its own government, the devil would be there to control it, as well; and to take this line of thinking even further: if the temple was in fact the place where many believed God lived, even symbolically as a house of God's residence at this point in history, so also does the devil lives there.

As it happens, Jesus, being God incarnate, finds himself at the pinnacle of the temple only when the devil takes him there. And when the devil makes him appear there, Jesus is at the mercy of the devil's magic, high up on top of the building, asking God himself to save himself from death, and Jesus, as God, says "no, thanks." As this is the first reading of our Sunday worship in this season of Lent, we begin with something quite interesting: *God says no to saving himself from death,* and we will end this season with God himself dying on a cross.

I can't help but connect this scene to the story of Adam and Eve in the Garden of Eden. The devil approaches Jesus in the same way that the talking snake approaches Eve. The snake says to the first woman that she should eat of the fruit of the Tree of Knowledge of Good and Evil, assuring her, "You shall not die" for eating the fruit, for when you eat of the fruit, "you will be *like God,* knowing good and evil" (Gen. 3:4–5).

Jesus is taken to the highest point of the Temple in Jerusalem—the highest point of the center of the universe and the holiest place in the world—above the abode where God resides, and *there is where Jesus is tempted to be God.* Consider this: the devil is *tempting God to be a God,* but Jesus, as God, refuses this temptation to be God! This is the greatest story ever told!

\* \* \*

This past Monday we learned the somewhat surprising news that Pope Benedict XVI is resigning. Many people are kind of surprised or shocked that a Pope would, or could, resign, since if you have a billion people believing that you have the ability to infallibly speak for God, why would you ever resign? If you speak for God himself, to whom do you submit your resignation? It is actually Catholic doctrine that only the Pope himself can accept his own resignation.

The history of Popes resigning is interesting; other Popes resigned as a result of power struggles or to prevent a schism. One Pope, Benedict IX, who was one of the most corrupt Popes in history, was actually Pope three times during the years 1045–1046, after resigning and selling the office of the Pope. St. Celestine V was Pope for only five months in the year 1294 and actually made the process of a Pope resigning official law so that he could resign without dispute or claim to return, because he hated the job. I find it interesting that in 2009 Pope Benedict IX, who has just resigned, publically prayed at the tomb of Pope Celestine, who was the pope who made papal resignation law. The last time a Pope resigned was Pope Gregory XII, who resigned in 1415 to prevent schism in the church. Clearly, the Pope resigning is historically noteworthy.

The idea that the Pope is infallible is not an easy concept to trace through history, and likely begins in late medieval times. But we should remember that the infallibility of the Pope was not *formally declared* as official church teaching until the First Vatican Council, which occurred in 1870. For us Protestants, who don't quite understand Catholics' fascination with the Pope, and for us who stand as interested bystanders to all things surrounding the Pope, it is natural to ask: How is one infallible (if even under certain conditions) one day, and not the next? This doesn't make sense to us.

The poison of Protestantism has always been the fact that we Protestants emphasize the individual's interpretation of scripture, which leads to sometimes awful interpretations of scripture—from slavery, to the Holocaust, to Westboro Baptist Church, and everything in-between.

One time I was at a Costco in New Jersey and the man serving food there told me the history of his local church. They were Dutch Reformed, but their minister got in trouble for something, so the church split in half, and his church left the denomination and stayed with the minister. Later they split again over temperance and women's rights. Again, they split over whether the King James Version of the Bible was the only legitimate Bible or not. And then they split again over whether women could speak in the sanctuary or not—he called his group the "Liberal" faction because women are allowed to read from the Bible and make announcements in church now. But then he said they recently split again over some debate about how the end of the world is exactly going to happen—if you know your theology, some were "pre-tribulation," the others were what is called "post-tribulation"—and, the man told me, this most recent split was hard on the church.

I asked him how many people were left in the church. "About three families," he said. I asked if he was not related to any of them, and he said he is related to everyone in those schisms, but those three families are the only ones left that he associates with or talks to.

The problem with Protestantism is that because we have no Pope, we have no Big Heavenly Authority, no single authority that speaks for all of us; we often declare ourselves Pope. *We are the Pope of ourselves.* We all know the story of King Henry VIII who wanted a divorce from the Pope, and when the Pope wouldn't give it to him, he said, "Screw you, Pope, I'm now the Pope of this Island!" Hence, today, we have an Episcopal and Anglican Church. Part of the danger of Protestantism is that our belief system leads us to declare ourselves Pope.

We can have our disagreements about preferences for things in church, and some things are just cosmetic and our preferences are just that: preferences. But we make a mistake when we decide that my version of things is the only way, and that my interpretation of religion is The Truth.

And, of course, when we sin, and when we rebel against God, and when we participate in injustice, and when we give honor to kingdoms that we know answer only to the devil, and when we do not work for equality and justice and turn a blind eye to poverty and exploitation and the racism that is everywhere around us, *we declare ourselves Pope, and this declaration is the root of all human evil.* It is the root of all human evil from the tempting of the serpent in the Garden of Eden to the killing of Abel by Cain to the tempting of Jesus by the devil himself on the pinnacle of the temple. We will make excuses or justifications for our actions, but we know that we do it, we know that this drive to declare ourselves Pope is often at the core of our being, and we know that we all stand in need of constant repentance. To add further insult, when we act as our own personal Popes we find rituals and methods by which we pretend that we aren't the Pope, we make ourselves out to be victims, and we find a way to justify our actions. We might as well just get on our knees and openly pronounce our worship of Satan.

The Good News is that we are to follow the likeness of Christ. As Gil Bailie observes, Jesus, while God, is human, and these tests by the devil are serious tests, they "are not mock tests."[2] Jesus discloses his divinity *by denying his divinity* in the face of Satanic temptation. This is the path we are to follow, even and especially when the path follows through the Valley of Kidron, which is a valley in the shadow of death, the valley Jesus and the devil looked down upon from the pinnacle of the temple, the way of the tomb and the path between the Last Supper and the Garden of

Gethsemane. We are tempted and dealt serious situations, even if we are not magically taken to the top of the temple. But when we follow Jesus, we are to deny our temptation to be God, to declare ourselves Pope, and instead we are to radically humble ourselves.

Christians throughout history have known this as the Good News of Christ, and even while there are exemplary examples of Christians changing the world by taking up the cross, time and time again we as a Christian people have failed to follow the path of the cross. This is evident through any tour of history. Will we, in response, continue this long history of failure, and of declaring ourselves to be Pope, or will we as a restored people learn from the horror of history and, in an authentic and genuine way, take this Lenten journey of the cross with Jesus?

## Smelling Like Pig Slop and Loose Women
(Lent 4)
*Psalm 32; Luke 15:1–3, 11–32*

Most of us know this story of the lost Son or the prodigal Son. In fact, I was just thinking about this story as I was watching the Disney movie *Pinocchio* with my children a week or two ago. The scene in the movie where the boys, including Pinocchio, are taken away to Pleasure Island before they are kidnapped is especially disturbing to me, partially because it seems to have an undertone of how child molesters groom children they are about to abuse—to the point that it made me cringe watching this cartoon, *Pinocchio*. Consequently, in the movie the children are all turned into donkeys, which I think is symbol of the child abuse, after they are given a taste of alcohol and tobacco, representing in the addictions that adults have, offering them to children as a kind of forbidden fruit.[1]

The other thing that Pinocchio reminds me of in this story is what Pinocchio is most famous for, which is the lying. In our Bible story, the youngest son exploits the father's money, returns home and is extravagantly welcomed back. I can imagine his nose getting larger as he is lying. In fact, the Father sees the son coming home from a distance, and the son begins delivering the speech he had been rehearsing on his way home. The Son had rehearsed this whole speech about how the father's servants were eating better and so on, but the Father was so happy that he didn't even let him give the sad speech. All the Son said was "Father, I've sinned against God, I sinned before you, I don't deserve to be called your son ever again."

Of course, the father welcomes him home, puts good clothes on his son, places a ring on his finger, and calls a banquet. This part of the story is important, because the ring is a symbol of the inheritance, the banquet here is a symbol of heaven, of the banquet that has no end.

The way I have always heard this story and the way I have always been taught to interpret this story places emphasis on the banquet at the end, that the prodigal son is an analogy or allegory about how God welcomes home sinners. I have actually heard this story preached at funerals for people who were pretty clearly not Christians as a mean to comfort the grieving, that God welcomes home everyone who returns. To be honest, I like this interpretation of the story, that no matter how far away we've gone from God, when we come back we are welcomed home. (In fact, to follow my connection to *Pinocchio* earlier, this theme is a lot like another Disney movie that some of you have surely seen, *Finding Nemo,* where the Father does everything he can to get his lost son back.)[2]

But then within the Bible story we have the older brother, who is not only jealous but upset. This brother did everything right and was always faithful, and probably wasn't unhappy that the younger brother returned, but the older brother probably felt that there was an injustice against himself happening here in the extremes by which the father was celebrating the younger brother's return. The father's response was that before the son was as good as dead, but he has now returned—*that's worth celebrating!*

\* \* \*

Something tells me that the older brother probably wasn't so convinced. We all know that there is a big difference between the older child and the younger child in a family, right? With the oldest child, the parents want to take the child to the doctor every time they sneeze, they are much stricter about enforcing the rules, and they are far more cautious about how they let the child go into the world. But when it comes to the youngest child the rules are more relaxed, there is a lot less hand-holding, and the youngest child generally gets away with a lot more. I remember as a college student that it was quite unfair that my father bought my brother a car. It wasn't a great car, it was a very used, very traveled Oldsmobile Delta 88 from the late 70; pretty snazzy for its age, it even had an 8-track player. But the thing was that my parents made me wait well beyond the point at which I was allowed to get a driver's license, but now my brother had a car. Most of us, if we are older children, have stories like this, whether they are real stories or how we perceive them.

From a psychological perspective, the youngest child usually is the "baby" of the family because the parents realize that this child is the last one who will call them "daddy" or "mommy" and the child never really gets out of their childhood in the eyes of the parents. Many of you surely have stories in your family of people for whom the coincidence of being the youngest child and the way the parents treated the youngest child affected that person for the rest of their lives.

Consequently, in the Bible story, the baby of the family comes home, smelling like pig slop and loose women, with a sad story, and saying to his father all the right things: My life doesn't mean anything to you, and it doesn't mean anything to God, and I want to be your slave, and I'm sorry. The older brother is hearing his father recount the story and the other brother moans, "we've heard *this* before, haven't we?" Isn't this the same speech you gave when you wrecked the old man's chariot?

The tension between the older brother and the younger brother is all over the Bible—beginning with Cain and Abel—so we should remember that *this* dimension of sibling rivalry is going on here, and the bottom line here is that the younger brother probably was being dishonest and was lying to his father. The older brother is listening in to the explanation and saying—*that's the biggest lie I've ever heard!* The older brother knows that the younger brother is lying, and says that the younger brother is *playing the old man like a fiddle*. The younger brother has said it all before, he's given all the excuses before: this is what is implied in the way Jesus tells this story, when coming home the brother was even reciting his rehearsed speech, which, of course, was interrupted by the father.

\* \* \*

It would seem that the father wasn't so smart, and that he got duped by the same son who had a history of exploiting the father; we should remember that it was the son who asked for his inheritance before the father was even dead! The first Christians interpreted Jesus' teaching on this particular point differently than we typically do. We know from early Christian writings that what the early church focused upon was that the older son represented the old-order Jews and the younger son represented the more liberal, generally younger Jews who came into the faith as converts rather than by birth. Those who converted broke the laws before they were Jewish, but then they expected to be equal with those who were born into the religion (who followed the law for their whole lives)—and sometimes the rules were bent by the priests to include the younger people more than might have been tolerated in the past.

Jesus' parable, therefore, was interpreted by the earliest Christians to be about the tension between generations within the faith community, how the older people like their rules and their traditions and don't like to accommodate or make room for the newer and younger people. All faith communities face this struggle at some point, and we in this church are facing this right now in some ways as we talk about growth, knowing that history always shows that religions and churches that do not adapt and do not change do not grow. Giving the ring to the younger son suggests that whether the older generation likes it or not, the younger will outlive them with or without the temple or the church. Whether the older generation likes it or not, the younger generation is the future of the temple.

In this interpretation the focus is taken away from the banquet at the end of the story, on which we so often place our emphasis, as the feast typically represents the next life; rather, the focus here is the duped father placing the ring on the son's finger. In other words, the father isn't forgiving the son simply because he always has, and not simply because he is happy to be alive, even though he clearly is happy that he's still alive; and the father isn't only *forgiving* his son out of a legal obligation or out of a social concern that he should not take his own son as a slave—which, we should be clear, is what the manipulative son asks him to do as an insult to his own father—but that *forgiveness is implied simply by virtue of the fact that he is his son, no matter what.* The father does not give the son the opportunity to lie his way out because his lies, and even *the truth of what happened is largely irrelevant to the father.*

\* \* \*

We don't know if the son received an inheritance after the old man died, and the focus of Jesus's teaching in the parable is no longer about the justice or economics of the situation. But we can be assured that the son kept the ring as the outward sign of his inheritance—the same inheritance that he blew: the ring is symbolic in that even though the son burned through all of the inheritance, family is more important than money and that the son will always be the father's son.

We also don't know if the younger son ever disappointed the father ever again—my guess is that he probably did. The younger son might have complained years later that he never had equal treatment with the older son; most of us know how sibling rivalries go. We don't know if the younger son was ever sincere in his repentance. What we do know is that the father accepted him back, at least initially, and offered him a *welcome to prove himself worthy of the welcome.*

This is where I find meaning in the *reversal* of this parable. The father gives the younger son a family ring as a symbol of his inheritance and return welcome, and he essentially empowers the son to respond. It doesn't matter whether the son really was sorry when he got home, but he is now in a situation where *repentance must happen* with his hands and feet and not just with his mouth. The son can now live up to the family name or, he can take the ring off and walk away or, he can pawn it and go back to the liquor, the women, the gambling. The choice is whether to live up to the extravagant welcome or not.

\* \* \*

The line that strikes me the hardest is the verse in Jesus's parable where the son has some kind of epiphany, or realization, that after spending his money on wine, women, gambling, and who knows what else, he is sitting in pig slop, ready to eat the food given to the pigs. In fact, the exact language of the Bible is that he would eat the "pods" that the pigs were eating. A "pod" probably refers to the fruit of the carob tree, or carob pod, which was a common shrub throughout the Mediterranean region. Carob pods were probably a food people resorted to during extreme famine because the pods are eaten dry. During World War II, people in Malta began eating carob pods to ration scarce resources. Even though they are high in protein, they don't taste so good, but they last a long time. So in ancient times a farmer would have carob pods around for emergencies, or as a crop to sell during emergencies or famine, but if there was not a famine that year or extreme need, the pods would be fed to the pigs.

The subtext here is that when the son went away his money was not in a time of scarcity, but in a time of plenty, the economy was good, meaning that had he invested his money or used it wisely he might have prospered, and he was spending his money along with others who may have had money to burn because of the better than usual economic situation. He got caught up in the moment, and got caught up in thinking the money will never run out because he is living in the immediacy of the present, and the present is full of good times.

The other image that strikes me is the Jewish boy sitting in pig slop, contemplating eating food meant for the pigs, sitting around among pigs that are eating. Most people know that Jewish law prohibits the eating of pork because it is from an unclean animal. So this Jewish boy contemplates his fortunes sitting among animals who are designated to be unclean animals outside of kosher regulations, and he considers eating with them.

The whole situation, as a single image, is a good metaphor for where this boy finds himself—an outcast, not by birth, or an outcast not because of some sexual status like a eunuch, or an outcast not because of his family situation, or his race, etc., but *he is an outcast because of his choices.* He has no one to blame but himself for making bad choices. At rock bottom, as a total outcast, even from the people he threw money at (because he had no more money to throw), he can make the final choice to completely divorce himself from his identity as a member of God's chosen race and eat with the forbidden animals, and live in their slop. He could choose to reap what he has sown *or* he could choose to come back and at least be given some dignity as a human being or as a slave.

The Good News is that we could debate where the son experienced grace in this story, whether sitting in pig slop, or when his father embraces him, or ~~even~~ when the father enables him in the first place, or at the end of the story. But in truth, grace is found everywhere in the parable. The son's redemption and forgiveness is *gracefully* offered despite his sincerities. He experiences extravagant and *graceful* forgiveness, as his father throws a big party for him as a symbol for that *grace*. The son may fail again, but forgiveness is offered unconditionally. The son *has to allow himself to be honored as the special guest to the party,* a party that is not only just a party; it is a reality of the *grace-laden* community his father is trying to establish with him.

\* \* \*

In Jesus' story, the son is accepted by his father without any crucifixion, without any resurrection, and without any pretext of a messiah or rules read from some holy book—he doesn't even say the Sinner's Prayer! The father interrupts the son's rehearsed speech of repentance. The message is this: the forgiveness and grace of the father does not require repentance, and offers unconditional grace for no other reason than for *grace*. No amount of repentance or apology will ever be good enough. The apology or repentance itself is not as important as is the authentic desire simply to return, to be accepted, and to be bound back to the father.

We should remember that the word "religion" literally means to "rejoin," "reconnect," or "to be bound again." Sometimes when we bind ourselves to the cross, we get crucified—just ask anyone who has been in a leadership position in a church or on a school board. God does not require us to be crucified. Some religious folks bind themselves to the Bible, but sometimes binding oneself to scripture just becomes a narrow experience of life, one in which we cut off people from our families when they don't measure up to whatever Biblical standards we make up at any given time. Others bind themselves to an agenda; being part of the church is to be seen, or for business purposes, etc.

However, here we have Jesus telling a parable where being *bound to a community* is the result of a liberal dispensing of *grace*. The father's grace at the son's return did not come with money, but of an embrace. This is to say that we are bound as a community, no matter what we smell like, no matter where we've been and what we've done. Sometimes our families will not accept us: practicing the graceful community is not popular. It's worth noting that the faithful son was angry, but this is the point: the older son was in the wrong, too, because he was not practicing the graceful community, but wished for a community of vengeance, and a community of merits.

Our message in this church is that it's time to let God out of the cage and out of the prison in which we incarcerate God in with our rules and with our language. It is time to stop arguing about who is in and who is out in a Kingdom that we falsely believe to be under our own authority to decide. It is time to stop arguing about what minorities are not allowed in and who is to be kept out. It's time to proclaim loudly: "God is loose in the world and God will not be contained by your codes, your rituals, your rules, your institutions, your hierarchies."[3]

What does this risk of us? It makes us risk our comfort zones, our privileges, our rule books, our egos. We must risk our desire to get ahead and we must risk our desire to point out the smell on those returning home. We need courage to approach the risky areas where these questions hit the fan: What happens if I can't own so many guns? Will we have to find a new language for thinking about mental health and illness in our culture? Will we need a new awareness for thinking about race and education, and poverty and whiteness? Will this require me to find or invent a new language for my faith or for my desire to dispense grace and forgiveness, and to ask repentance, and acknowledge that words will never be enough for the love of God reflected upon us by this Jesus whom we claim to worship and know?

Many people in our culture, many in our families—*who are they? The ones who stay at home on Sunday mornings*—are asking: What's the point? Why bother with Christianity? I believe this is the answer. Imagine what this world would be like if we Christians who love to sing "Amazing Grace" began to *practice amazing grace*. What would this world be like if Christians practiced Christianity?

## The Resurrectionist
(Lent 5)
*Isaiah 43:16–21; Philippians 3:4b-14;*
*John 11:1–27, 38–44, 53–57, 12:1–11*

I've been reading a book titled *The Italian Boy,* by Sarah Wise, a book about the public exposure of the dark side of urban expansion in London in the early 1830s, namely, the business that emerged of body snatching.[1] Body snatchers were thieves who stole corpses from graves. The population of London exploded in the first three decades of the nineteenth century, and these years also saw an expansion of interest in the medical sciences and a new demand for medical workers.

To go back in time a little, fifty years prior, the English Parliament declared in the Murder Act of 1751 that the practice of "gibbeting" was expanded to allow judges to not only order an execution as punishment for murder, but that the executed corpse would be placed on display in a public place, usually along a highway or at a busy crossroads. The idea was to deter the growing problem of murders in London by treating the bodies of murderers in the same way the royalty would treat the bodies of those who commit treason against the King: traitors and pirates.

The following year, another Murder Act was passed by Parliament, the Murder Act of 1752. The Murder Act of 1752 was designed again to further deter murder crimes by making clear that those who commit murder will not be buried after execution, and that their remains must be either displayed by gibbeting, with the body publicly hanging in chains, or—and this is the innovation—the body will be turned over to scientists for "public dissection." As a result, the bodies of those convicted of murder could be turned over to medical colleges for use in teaching.

With the expansion of medical education and research, however, there were not enough felons whose bodies ended up on the dissection tables. As a result, a somewhat lucrative black market emerged for fresh bodies to be sold in secret to medical colleges. Body snatchers or corpse thieves became known as "resurrectionists," who would steal the bodies from freshly dug graves. There is even some evidence that medical students became involved with grave robbery, using the money they would receive for stealing the corpses to pay for their medical classes where they would be supervised in the dissection of the same bodies. Those who made their livings as resurrectionists were known to be making good money and were part of a new middle class that emerged in early 19th century London.

Younger men who wanted to learn the trade secrets of grave robbery even paid other professionals to train them. Resurrectionists who were experienced could open a traditional grave and be on their way in 30 minutes, and paid gratuities to church sextons, local officials, cemetery security, police, and informants to get away with their theft. Doctors and medical professors would not cooperate with the law because doing so would limit the number of students the colleges could enroll. Furthermore, the law usually took a blind eye to grave robbing, because their crime was only the destruction of property—the grave itself, since the body technically belonged to no one. If caught, resurrectionists might have been whipped, but generally speaking the law looked the other way.

The mortuary industry responded to try to deter body thieves. Instead of closing a grave with dirt, graves were filled with stones to deter people trying to dig them out. Family members would watch a grave at night for long enough that the body would be worthless for sale. This led to resurrectionists actually constructing tunnels, and sometimes systems of tunnels, through cemeteries and pulling out graves from the sides rather than from the top of the coffins. In response, coffin designers tried all sorts of things, including finding ways to buckle the deceased into a coffin using iron straps, and even burying coffins in iron cages, some of which were so large they rose above ground level as a signal to resurrectionists not to even try to exhume this grave. For those who could not afford these kinds of devices and contraptions, resurrectionists countered by paying professional mourners to pose as family members of the deceased in cemeteries to tip them off to the schedules of family members coming and going from graves and to be lookouts for other family members.

This all came to a head when two Irishmen, William Burke and William Hare, committed a series of murders to sell to a physician. After Burke was executed, his body was given to science for dissection by order of the judge. Instead of deterring people from body-snatching, the execution had the opposite effect: even more entered the resurrectionist business because it came out publically how much money was made from the business. This increased activity soon led to the public discovery of organized group of body snatchers when King's College School of Anatomy reported to police that a resurrectionist attempted to deliver the body of a boy who looked as if he was murdered. Other murders were then reported by grave robbers. Parliament then passed a law called the Anatomy Act of 1832 which required anatomy teachers to be licensed and that along with the unclaimed dead, prisoners and others may elect their bodies to be given to science, sometimes in exchange for their bodies to be properly buried after being used for science. Donating one's body to science for the poor was a way to receive something involving a middle-class burial.

Now, what does this have to do with our long Bible readings today? Our reading from Isaiah 43 says, "I am about to do a new thing; now it springs forth, do you not perceive it?" This sense of "perception" is for me the sense of smell: When it rains in the spring, is there not a new smell in the air? You can not only smell the pavement or the macadam after a spring rain; but you can also smell the life bursting out all around you. The New Creation is not just something we see, but something we smell, and something we can taste in the air, just as we can taste spring coming if we open our nostrils up and go beyond what we simply see and hear.

Old things have a smell, too. In Philippians 3, while talking about his sacrifice of all things on account of this new life in Christ, Paul says he has "suffered the loss of all things and I regard them as *rubbish*." That which is of the old ways, those things of the past, is "rubbish"; sometimes in other translations of the Bible it is translated as "garbage." The Greek word here is *skubala,* which is not just trash, but is the Greek word for *shit.* This word is also used in the book of Sirach, written about 200 years before, as waste different than manure, and is clearly a vulgar, slang word used for human excrement.[2] The point is that the *old* smells like *shh-skubala,* and the new smells like, the New. We can tell when something is old or when something is new with our noses.

In our Jesus story, Jesus goes to the tomb of Lazarus, whose body has been decomposing for four days, and when the tomb is opened, the crowd is offended by the stench of death. This is the smell of the old. Jesus does not retreat but enters the tomb of death and revives Lazarus not just to life, but to new life, a new life that is touched by the love and compassion of God through Jesus.

Later, while Jesus is eating in the home of Lazarus, Mary takes what the Bible says is "costly perfume made of pure nard," and "anointed Jesus' feet," wiping his feet with her hair. What the Greeks called "nard" is what we today would call lavender; and the smell was said to fill the whole house. The smell of New Life was this expensive perfume. Judas immediately quips that the nard was wasted and the money should have been given to the poor, and Jesus defends her, welcoming her blessing and hospitality, and making an allusion that this nard would be used to preserve Jesus' body for death.

If we are to read the Gospel of John seriously, we know that later a character named Nicodemus provides the burial agents for Jesus,[3] but we can see this episode as Jesus foreshadowing his death and that being blessed by the women is preparing him for his death.

But there is more to this. Those hearing the Gospel of John would have known that nard was not an agent used for burial. Nard or "spikenard" is mentioned a few times in the Hebrew Bible as "ketoret" or altar incense described in Exodus, Leviticus, 1 and 2 Chronicles.[4] This ketoret, or mixture of spices, would have been brought by everyone in the congregation together to be burned as part of the sacrifices offered on the altar for the worship of God, a practice that began early with the Jews and continued into the period of the Second Temple, the temple that was destroyed shortly before the Gospel of John was written.

The point of this is to say that with the temple gone, there was nowhere to sacrifice your spices and perfumes. By wiping the flesh of Jesus' feet with nard, Mary is performing an act of total submission to Jesus' flesh as the new altar of God. With nowhere else left to genuinely worship God, the flesh of Jesus' feet is all that is left; she worships his flesh with her most costly perfume and with her hair.

The symbolism of this story is that the perfume of the nard is not just symbolic of Jesus' eventual death, but symbolic that Jesus is the living God standing before them. This dichotomy of life and death is precisely what Paul's writing is attempting to underscore. The old life is "old," and the new life is "new," even if I am living one continuous life: I do not need to die to experience the love and acceptance of Christ, because I can worship and experience God *now,* in this world, and experience God through the flesh of Jesus and in my own flesh, and give praise and honor God through my senses, especially my sense of smell.

But now to push this even further: nard would have also been understood by the Jews hearing and reading the Gospel of John as a somewhat common spice that was used in Roman cuisine during ancient times.[5] In other words, Mary is not only wiping Jesus' feet with nard as an act of worship, and as a symbolic act of preparation for burial, but also as spicing his flesh to be consumed. Just as John the Baptists' head was served on a platter, presented as food before the local Roman imperialist representative, Jesus is making the case that he is being prepared to be similarly executed as the enemy of the Roman Empire. Except, as we know, Jesus reverses this symbolism and he presents to us his body and blood to consume, as we are empowered as the enfleshed remnants of God, through the Holy Spirit, to enact justice and the Kingdom in the here and now.

So when Lazarus is called out of his tomb, he is not simply resurrecting life into a body that is dead, but the entire scene of death is interrupted and inverted. It is quite likely that the reason why a crowd had gathered there was because there were mourners attending other graves, and some were actually professional mourners, people who were paid to sit in graveyards. There is evidence of this mentioned in the Bible as a Jewish practice, but it was common throughout ancient cultures in the Near East. The mourners were there for the money, and even the poorest families might have felt pressure to have at least one professional mourner present, crying, and praying, and singing. We have probably felt the experience of going to a funeral and not too many people showing up— the first funeral I officiated was a man with no family who died in prison. It was just me, the Muslim prison chaplain from another jail, and men from a lower security prison there to dig the hole in the cemetery lying beyond the state prison. On that day we were all professional mourners, we all had a job to do. Professional mourners were often highly trained in ritual and scripture, and were hired to ensure there was a proper burial.

So who among the living gathered at the tomb is he interrupting? It is worth noting that Jesus orders "them," as in those in the crowds, the professional mourners, to assist the raised Lazarus out of the tomb. Imagine how this made the professional mourners react! Here comes along this guy into my workplace—God knows who he is!—and he starts raising people from the dead? Not only is this religiously suspicious but he is going to put the professional mourners out of business!

So word gets out—back of course to the religious zealots who plot to kill Jesus and later, to, of all things, kill Lazarus, who had just been rescued from death!

\* \* \*

We live in a culture of death, do we not? The more we learn and discover about our past, the more we realize that our culture is not one that has always been a noble source of life—to the point that we resort to stealing the dead to make a living. And it is inevitable that stealing the dead leads to murdering others, and then children, simply to make a living. But we don't need to use these analogies, or look that far to see the *lust for death* that surrounds us everywhere: from the war machine to the poverty machines we support and endorse through ours and other governments, to the exploitation we see of children though the way their clothing commodifies their bodies, clothing made by children exploited by capitalism on the other side of the planet!

The philosopher Nietzsche said of his religious culture that all he could see around him was the stench of death, but it was not just the overwhelming stench of death in culture—it was the decomposition of God.[6] When we look the other way of injustice, and do not love our neighbor, and when we sell God out for silver and gold, and when we posture a care for the poor but yet do nothing, we are participating in the pervasive death that surrounds us.

The Good News is *not* that if we believe that Jesus is the answer, that we are saved. The Good News is that it is not ever enough just to believe; our call and challenge is to *act*. We can believe all day that Jesus brings about a New Creation and saves us from death and brings us into new life, but we know that this is what we call "cheap grace." The Way of the Cross, which is the way of God, is one of self-sacrifice, and denial, and practicing what we preach. It is to bring hope to places that have none, it is bring new life into realms of death—through small gestures and big events. Both small and large actions and life-giving speech have the power to change the world. Just smiling at someone can have a tremendous, transformative power. Speaking radically against injustice can change the world and inspire others to take up the cross for the world.

Jesus is teaching us how we are to encounter Easter when we discover it. When we open the tomb, that is to say, when we encounter death, we are not to come out of the tomb and parade our religion. In fact, Jesus got out of dodge after raising Lazarus, as he was a marked man because he had interrupted the celebration of death upon which so many people thrived. Jesus is showing us how to encounter Easter by teaching us how to encounter death, namely, that the encounter of death for those of us who are given New Life through water and the Spirit is that death is to declare this death to be a building block of the Kingdom of God that is total life, that is new life. This death is rendered only to be a transitional point for my contribution to this Kingdom, which is a kingdom of life that triumphs over the kingdom of death.

Those who mourn over death are to be blessed, Jesus says in the Sermon on the Mount.[7] But those who practice death, and live death, and participate in the culture and apparatuses of death, which exist all around us, are now *interrupted,* and offered a *reversal of course.* Jesus says, famously, "the poor will always be with you, but you will not always have me." This is not to justify poverty but to acknowledge that those who lust for death will always be the ones in power and the ones who seek power. The Empire must fall, but *not the Empire alone.* History has shown that we have rarely seen sparks of this life in our celebration of death throughout the centuries, and all around us. Jesus was right: those who *lust for life* are few and far-between.

My friends, as we come into these last weeks of Lent, of Palm Sunday, and Holy Week, and lead into Easter, let us not forget that these events and stories are not simply stories, and not simply historical accounts. Rather, these are blueprints for the Kingdom of God. We can watch the world passively, ~~and~~ complain about the death reigning all around us, and retreat into church for a pat on the back and reassurance that we're earning our piece of Heavenly Real Estate. We know this is not Christianity, yet we know this is how it is often practiced. Or we can follow these footsteps of Jesus, these footsteps still perfumed exquisitely and strongly by the hairs of a prostitute, and use our words, our actions, our hands and our feet, our wealth and our privilege, to finally begin this process of the cross, this process of Easter that was initiated so long ago, and *be* the crucifixion and *be* the Easter that Jesus so boldly demonstrated to us.

## How we Kill God[1]
(Lent 5, RCL)
*John 8:1–11*

Jesus is walking to Jerusalem from the Mount of Olives, which is the small mountain or hill just opposite of the Temple, and begins teaching, and a crowd forms. The lawyers and the Pharisees bring a woman caught in adultery to Jesus. The lawyers were kind of like the fundamentalist investigators for groups that are in power, probably the Sadducees or the priests, who were wealthy or had religious or political power. Their loyalty was to the written law of the Torah, but more importantly, their social role was to get people scared that the lawyers would report someone back to their bosses who had power.

As a result, the lawyers could force one to become ostracized, or one's business to be condemned, or children to be oppressed or repressed. Even worse, in the most extreme situations, one could find oneself being stoned as a result of their accusations. The lawyers might get people upset enough that they would get one's own townspeople to mob stone someone in their own town or their own family—so the lawyer would supposedly remember or report who took the side of the law back to his bosses. Here we have a lawyer doing just this. He interrupts Jesus' teaching, maybe with some rocks to throw, and brings an adulterous woman to stone.

The Pharisees are often perceived by modern readers to also be the religious conservatives, but "conservative" might not be the right term here. The Pharisees who believed that everyone should live their lives as if they were the privileged priests of the Temple. They didn't believe that everyone should actually be priests, but that everyone, or at least all men especially, should learn how to read scripture, and how to interpret it, and live a life of holiness like what is ascribed to the lives for priests in the Temple. The real Temple priests saw this group as a threat, but they tolerated this group insofar as they didn't threaten their power or authority. But the Pharisee showing, up in the middle of Jesus' teaching with an adulterous woman, suggesting that Jesus initiates the first stone, is in doing so asking Jesus to interpret the scriptures in such a way that Jesus would personally condemn her *with the authority* of a priest.

The lawyer provokes a situation which places Jesus in an either/or conundrum. Jesus can either stone the woman or not stone the woman—but if Jesus doesn't stone the woman, the crowd might retaliate against Jesus, and stone him, for not following the laws of scripture. Conversely, the Pharisee attempts to force Jesus to make a judgement call about scripture: if Jesus says to stone the woman, or to not stone the woman, either pronouncement from a place of authority would be seen as Jesus elevating his station to be higher than the priests in the temple. The Pharisees believed that everyone should live like priests, but likely not to the point of making *actual* judgments on others, as if they were the *real* priests. I hope you see the tense situation being painted by this story.

The woman is brought before Jesus, and the two instigators ask, in verse 8:4, "Teacher, this woman was caught in the act of adultery, in the law, Moses commanded us to stone women like this, what say you?"

We don't know where this woman came from or whether she really was adulterous. Nor do we know whether the other one involved in the adulterous affair was there, or who he was. The tradition here is that the adulterous woman was a prostitute, which is why no man is being brought forth here, which would paint a picture of all of the men there as being complicit or even her own clients. We don't know.

That being said, the way this story is typically interpreted is as the introduction of Mary Magdalene, a follower of Jesus who is described elsewhere in the Gospel of John after this. She is the woman saved by Jesus, perhaps a prostitute, who is admonished by Jesus in verse 11 to sin no more.

The woman is brought to Jesus and he is challenged to make a pronouncement. According to the Torah, as the lawyer and Pharisee say, she is required to be stoned for adultery; in Leviticus 20 and Deuteronomy 22, those who are guilty of adultery are to be executed. However, the Torah says that *both* the adulterer and the adulteress are to be executed, not just one. But this isn't how the law was typically practiced—women would be shamed in public, and men would bring women to trial for arbitrary reasons, and often without evidence.

Public ruling on adultery would be practiced as an act of mob justice by a kangaroo court of men who would take other men at their word, so that when their wives or mistresses were threatening them with being charged with adultery, they could turn around and make an accusation, thereby eliminating the women. Especially in the countryside, this was practiced without representation of the government or the Temple. Women were afraid to challenge the practice, the commonplace system of patriarchal violence simply continued.

But in our Jesus story, there is a representative of the temple present. For Jesus to follow the scripture, again, he would be declaring himself to be something he is not. In verse 6, the Bible says, that they did this to find a reason to bring an accusation against him.

Jesus bends down and physically protects the woman accused of committing adultery, and gives his famous teaching, "whoever hasn't sinned should throw the first stone." Jesus did not say, "don't throw the stone"; Jesus didn't call them out for being hypocrites; Jesus didn't command them to follow the old Levitical codes to execute her. Jesus protects the one who is vulnerable, and turns the question to the male spectator-participants: *if you really are innocent, throw the stone and kill me first.*

Jesus substitutes himself for the one who is condemned, the one who is the scapegoat of the sins of people, especially men. For them to throw the stone, they would be throwing the stone at Jesus, with whom they have no scriptural or legal reason to kill. For the crowd to follow the biblical code, and to follow the persuasion of the mob mentality, they would have to kill someone who is innocent, or at least innocent of the crime of which they are administering justice under the law for, that is, adultery. The crowd would have to kill someone who is innocent to get to the one who they really intend to kill.

They all walk away.

The story ends again with Jesus admonishing the woman and telling her to sin no more.

\* \* \*

This story is interesting on a couple different levels, and not just because of its obvious teaching that Christians are not to be the ones standing in judgment over other people, especially in a situation where the one who is being accused or scapegoated hasn't done anything to them. I don't think this means that Christians shouldn't be judging the world or passing judgment on the world, but judging people themselves, and hurting people who have absolutely nothing to do with them, or scapegoating those in society who are often pointed to as the problem, when their elimination is really for the gain of those in power.

Beyond this, in most Bibles one will find a little footnote at the bottom of the page that states that this entire story, from John 7:53 to John 8:11, isn't found in the most ancient authorities of the scriptures, and scholars are in general agreement that this story probably did not happen in a literal way, and was added into the story of Jesus much, much later. The Gospel of John was not written by one single person, and it was written over a period of several decades by a group of people; John was not written to be read as a literal historical account. But here we find something suspicious with the archeological evidence of the text, namely, that it is missing, and that even our earliest writings on scripture omit any discussion of it or make any reference. Even some of our earliest writing on this passage of scripture questions the authenticity of the story.

To consider this Bible story in context, right before it, Jesus is speaking to those outside of the city for the Jewish holiday of the Festival of Booths. For example, beginning in John 7:37, the following discourse takes place on the last day of the Festival of Booths, which is a holiday where Jews slept outdoors in booths for a week to remember the forty years the Israelites wandered the desert with Moses. So Jesus is speaking to a group of Jews who were likely outside of the Holy City, on the outskirts of the city.

Some Bibles will add a subject header after the story of the stoning of the woman, between John 8:11 and 8:12, which reads "Jesus continues to teach in the temple." There is no indication that any of this would have taken place in the temple; the series of discussions happening in the text is presented as having happened *outside* during this time where the Jews remembered Moses being with them during a time following their captivity in Egypt. The implication here is that Jesus stands in for Moses as the new leader while speaking to the Jews. Doing so might make Jesus seem anti-Jewish, so affirms his Jewishness in 8:31–33, teaching that "the truth will set you free."

The image I get from reading this story is that Jesus is walking along the path from the booths or tents outside of the city to the temple inside of the city while giving these talks, and he gets more and more radical, and the crowd gets more and more outraged. Symbolically, the image is that Jesus goes from the memory of the Jews trusting in God with Moses in the desert to the spiritually dead location of the temple, with all of its corruptions. The religion has become sick and has become about who is outside, rather than who is inside. The practice of religion is about discrimination, and justifying discrimination, rather than the inclusive love of God.

Traveling this path from the tents of the Festival of Booths to the temple would have been a very typical way of Jews practicing the holiday in Jerusalem. The connection is to be made that once your people were homeless, following God in the wilderness, and now you have a home and a set place of worship and center of life in the temple. Jesus' point is that the temple isn't really the center of God; rather, God is everywhere and with all people.

John 8 ends with Jesus' most stunning statement yet, in 8:54ff., proclaiming that he has personal knowledge of Abraham, which is challenged by the crowd. In 8:58 Jesus says that even though he is obviously existing in the present, he also existed in the past; and further, he existed before the time of Abraham.

This was a final apostasy and the crowd had enough. In 8:59, the crowd gets ready to stone Jesus to death for saying something so heretical.

But Jesus went into hiding, and the Bible says, *Jesus left the temple.* A stoning like this wouldn't have happened inside of the temple, but perhaps outside of it. A big crowd would have been assembled from people coming to the temple from their tents outside of the city.

This is all to say, again, that the story of the woman being stoned doesn't quite fit in with the rest of the story, that this wouldn't have happened at the temple, and it seems out of order.

So back to the story of the adulterous woman. Why would this story be added in?

The tradition of the interpretation of the Bible has always recognized that certain things in the Bible were added to the text after it was completed. The ending of the Gospel of Mark is perhaps the best example of such an addition. Contemporary Bibles sometimes identify these parts that were added, and add little notes in fine print pointing these instances out. The fact that there are things added to the Bible is often a case made to discredit the stories and to even discredit the entire story of the Bible. I think it would be helpful here to consider the origin of the story.

\* \* \*

There was a philosopher named Apollonius of Tyana, who was born around the year 1 AD, and died around the year 98 AD, having spent most of his life in Ephesus. There is an unknown period in his life which we don't know about, from his childhood until his early 30s, where it's speculated that he went to India to learn the ways of the Hindus. He returned and became a student of Pythagoreanism, which was the religion that came out of the philosopher Pythagoras, who believed that numbers were the ultimate reality of the world.

The stories of Apollonius of Tyana are full of miracle stories and legendary magical feats. In fact, so similar are the stories of Jesus and Apollonius that there has always been a belief in the Western world that Apollonius of Tyana was really Jesus, or that the two had some contact, or that Jesus was a student of Apollonius, or that Apollonius was a teacher of Jesus. Some artwork has been found depicting Apollonius from long ago even calling him "Apollonius the Nazarene," believing that he really wasn't from Tyana, in Asia Minor, but from the village of Nazareth, as was Jesus.

But one of the most famous teachings of Apollonius is a perplexing one, but it should also sound a little familiar.

There was a terrible plague in Ephesus, and no matter what was done there was no remedy to it, and a significant chunk of the population was killed, and there was no end in sight. Since Apollonius, like Jesus, was known to be a healer, he was summoned by the people to do something, or to enact some miracle to stop the mass death that was all around them.

The people found Apollonius, and he proclaimed that he could heal them. So the entire crowd of the remaining living of the town followed Apollonius into the temple, which was a temple to Hercules (who is another story whose mythology is very similar to Jesus' story). The temples then were open air temples, so you could see outside, and just as they were before the idol of Hercules, an old man was walking by the temple, outside.

Apollonius pointed to the old man, walking along with his cane. The man was a beggar that had seen around town before, he was dressed in rags, he was clearly poor, he carried a small wallet with a little crust of bread in it. He looked hungry, and he looked like one of the last of this world. Apollonius pointed to the man and ordered the crowd to pick up any stones they could find and to hurl them at the man, saying that this man was the enemy of the gods and the cause of their disease.

The people refused. They wanted to believe Apollonius, but the solution that he offered to their problem was one they could not accept, that this beggar was the cause of their problems.

Apollonius provoked and taunted the crowd, saying again and again that they needed to stone this man, as the crowd surrounded the old beggar, who crouched down and covered his head with his thin arms, begging for mercy.

Then someone threw the first stone. And then a silence followed. And then a second stone, and immediately a third, fourth, and fifth stone. The stones came faster and faster to the man, until all of the remaining stones were thrown simultaneously. All of the Ephesians tried to outdo each other and the more stones they threw the easier it was to throw them.

As the stoners became intoxicated with the violence they were enacting, and as it became easier for them to believe that the old beggar was the cause of the disease, the man's eyes lit up like fire, like a demon full of rage. They crowd did not stop until a pile of stones appeared on top of and around the dead man that lay on the ground.

Apollonius moved the stones off of the body of the animal, and as he uncovered the body they discovered not a man but a demonic animal the size of the largest lion. This dead demon lay beaten to a pulp by the stones of the mob. The plague, as it happened, ended.

Afterwards, a new idol to Hercules was placed over the spot where the crowd had listened to the wise philosopher and killed the man who caused their plague.

The point of this awful story of Apollonius of Tyre was to emphasize the difficulty of casting the first stone. It's kind of like you're a kid and you come to a creek and everyone is exited to jump in the creek but no one wants to go first. Someone has to go first, which gives permission to everyone else to imitate the first. In our story, it took a while for someone to cast the first stone, because there was no one to imitate. But then it became easier and easier to cast the stones.

And the more and more they threw the stones, the more real the one believed to be the cause of their problems became the cause of their problems. As a kind of myth, we can deduce that we know that disease and problems of society is not caused by the poor. But any listen to our elected leaders makes pretty clear who the problems in our society are: the poor, the welfare recipient, the homeless, the sick, the disabled, and children whose parents are any of these. If the poor would just go away, somehow there would be more money to spend building a bigger military.

But the more and more we cast stones at the poor, the immigrant, the sick, the easier it is to do so, and the more someone says something or does something to cast the first stone, it is permission for everyone else to do so, saying, "finally someone has the guts to speak the truth." The more they are demonized and dehumanized to the point of becoming the wild animal that is the predator and the king of the jungle. The predator is killed by those who believe themselves to be the victims.

We see this all the time in our culture, in fact, some of our greatest feats of literature and film explore this entirely. This is what I really think Herman Melville's classic book, *Moby Dick,* is about, the search for that elusive whale which really causes no problems if left alone but is believed to be too dangerous, and too valuable, to leave it be. The whale is the scapegoat. Or the movie *Jaws,* and if you've not seen *Jaws* for a while now is the good time to watch it when you're not going to go to the beach for a while. The wild beast of the sea becomes an allegory to that which we blame all of our problems upon. And no matter how many times the shark in *Jaws* is killed, the shark keeps coming back, remember the tagline for *Jaws 2?* "This time, it's personal."

\* \* \*

Our story of Jesus halting a stoning may have been added into the text of John as a *reversal* of the similar story of Apollonius of Tyre. Apollonius was teaching that the way out of your problems is to agree upon what is the root cause, and kill it, even if it really isn't the root cause, the effort will solve your problems. And this is what we do in our culture all the time.

Jesus, on the other hand, defends the woman, who may or may not have been an adulteress, by placing his own body in front of her, and he writes something on the ground—perhaps a reference to the importance of the spot outside of the temple in Apollonius' story, the only place or evidence of Jesus writing anything down, and *reverses* the teaching of Apollonius, saying, in John 8:7, "Let anyone who is without sin cast the first stone."

For the first time the mob, as individuals and groups heard someone in a position of privilege—in this case, someone who had a crowd following him, stand up for the victim, and *put himself in harm's way to undo the logic of scapegoating violence.* The people gathered were hoping to have a good stoning that day.

The people were waiting for someone to throw the first stone to imitate. Instead, by examining themselves they imitated not someone enacting violence but began to imitate Christ, that is, by prioritizing the last of this world, in this case, a woman who may have been guilty or not, but the story obviously points to the fact that the sexuality of women, back then as it is today, becomes the site of blame and scapegoating for many of the problems of our world. Just listen for how we talk about abortion or teenage pregnancy, or seeing a teen doing something wrong in culture, asking "Where is that kid's mother?" or asking "Where is that kid's father?" as a way of blaming women for single motherhood.

Jesus stops the stoning, and then, walking to the temple with the crowd, implicates all of the men who participate in this ritual dance between blaming the victims of society and rendering themselves blameless with their religious practices of purifying themselves and believing themselves to be perfect. The story makes sense within the thematic content of John 8, which then ends with Jesus being the one who is scapegoated when they attempt to stone him. The point is that everyone showed up for a stoning that didn't happen, but they get their revenge on Jesus later in the story when he is executed by the state on the cross as the ultimate victim, the outsider on death row.

\* \* \*

So what does this all mean? We know we scapegoat and blame the victims of our society. We even admit that we do it while we do it, or we find backhanded ways to pretend we're not doing it when we're doing it, but we are only fooling ourselves.

When Jesus, who is God, points out how the logic of mob rule, and mob mentality exposes not the blame of the woman as the problem of society, but that this logic of blaming the victim ultimately calls us all to the carpet to realize that we victimize ourselves, and we victimize others to obscure the fact that we are to blame for our own problems, and that we are responsible for our own actions and situations. We can play a blame game as much as we want, and we can make it feel like we're not blaming anyone, but Jesus *interrupts the scene.* Jesus protects the victim, and, I like to think, holds up a mirror to the crowd, saying, whoever is without sin should cast the first stone.

Seeing themselves in the mirror, they walk away, for now. God or magicians or prophets of God do not swoop in to point the finger at who is the problem of society, which is what we see happening in the terrible story of Apollonius of Tyre. But in the story of Jesus, we see a God who discloses Godself by disclosing ourselves, and teaches that when we do cast that first stone, we are not only hurting ourselves, but we hurt others, but before any of that, we act to hurt God, who is the God of the victim. We seek to kill God, and when we do this, as the philosopher Nietzsche wrote, we become the murderers of all murderers. When we blame the victim, we might as well crucify God himself.

And, as we know, that's what happened.

The power of the cross is not just in its symbol of triumph of life over death. The real power of the cross is its humbling disclosure of *how we kill God, how we crucify God,* and how we make this world a continuation of crucifixion by looking into the mirror that Jesus holds up for us, and seeing ourselves, we cannot handle the truth of Jesus, so we cast the first stone, or simply follow the mob.

The cross represents this untying of the demand to blame victims, and to examine ourselves. When we live out this crucifixion, which is our call as Christians, to take up our own cross, we point to ourselves as the source of our own problems, in the hope that such bold and humble acts, which sometimes hurt us and punish us, will lead others to lay down their stones, and to imitate you imitating Christ.

## The World is Crucifixion
(Lent 6)
*Exodus 12:1–14, Luke 22:1–23*

During the time I worked as a prison chaplain intern, the state conducted one execution. On the day of the execution, I was not to come to work because I was considered inessential staff for the day, and I was forbidden to be on the premises of the prison outside, as I was obligated not to participate in any protest of an execution held at the facility where I was working.

I did not know the man who was executed, though I did talk to him briefly a week before he was executed—I was doing some rounds on the state's "X-Row," that's what they called Death Row there, and I remember meeting him, because about a month before the execution date extra guards are placed on the individual to make sure he does not try to commit suicide. I do know that he asked for his final meal to be a cheeseburger and fries from McDonald's.

Death Row at the prison was called "X-Row" for a couple reasons. First, every unit where prisoners were held had different unit names, after a letter of the alphabet. I was primarily responsible for units D and F, which were easier units because the inmates had to be on good behavior for several years to get into those units. Those units were cheaper to staff and offered a little more freedom than traditional cell blocks—these units were open-air with 4 foot walls separating small areas for the inmates to sleep, but there were no bars between them and it was more social.

The cable television show *America's Toughest Prisons* profiled this prison once. The show mentioned that this prison has the largest cell block in the country, which was an old, noisy, and hot unit, probably a half-mile long, where all of the bars were opened and closed by a wheel at the end of each floor, cranked by hand by an officer.[1] These two cell blocks were called A and B.

Death row was called unit "X," but was also called X because the sign above the outside entrance it looked like the symbol of the Skull and Crossbones. It was all about death.

I helped run a small group in the chapel in the prison, and one of the inmates made an interesting observation to me. He said that the whole prison was X-Row. This was a prison where the worst of the worst were housed, and where prisoners from lesser security prisons with severe mental disorders were sent. Few convicts ever walk out of this level-4 security prison—if you are not sentenced to death you are sentenced to life, or several life sentences. Most of these men were rapists, child molesters and murderers, or criminals from other prisons who became violent under prison conditions.

The inmate said to me that everyone there is serving a death sentence, whether the act of execution is carried out by the state or not. The whole prison is living in a culture of death. This conversation, I will add, was prompted by the fact that the warden ordered the only two trees in the whole prison to be cut down—these were trees outside of the chapel that were planted by inmates in memory of officers who were killed in a riot about ten years before. The warden said that these trees, which were no taller than a person, were too dangerous and ordered them to be taken out. This angered the inmates, and the chaplains, who felt that these trees were the only signs of natural life anywhere in the prison, and were planted as an act of reconciliation.

I suggested to the inmate that the X in "X-Row" is a Christian symbol. Some early Christians were crucified on an X-shaped cross. Many of the inmates were aware of Malcolm X, who was a Muslim but was a civil rights leader who rejected the internal and intentional racism of many Islamic groups in the mid-twentieth century.[2] They also related to the symbol of the "X" because many of them read old comic books that were donated to the prison and were familiar with *The Uncanny X-Men*, a comic book that was very much a way of responding positively to the civil rights movement of the 1960s.[3]

As we kept talking, the other inmates started discussing the culture outside of prison, that most people don't realize just how much of our culture is a culture of death, one that masks the horror of what is really happening in the world with feel-good religion, saccharine popular culture, and lies in the news. Another prisoner said, that *this* is what it means when we say that in Christ there is no Jew nor Greek, male or female, that Christ was crucified for everyone, whether we're in prison or not. You see, he said, it's easy for us in prison to say that we're victims of a larger system that is corrupt, but the fact is we say this because our own sin and corruption landed all us here, into a maximum-security prison, with the toughest criminals in the state.

But, he said, I wouldn't have found Christ in my life had I not ended up in prison, and I give thanks that I was finally punished before I did something even worse. Had I never been caught, I would have never found Jesus, and I wouldn't ever be able to tell anyone else about Jesus. And, the prisoner remembered from studying Greek that the word "Christ" actually begins with what we would call the letter X, which makes the *ch-* sound in Greek. (This is why we sometimes write "Merry X-Mas" at Christmas, because X was the first letter of the word Christ, and a way the early Christians abbreviated the word "Christ.")

\* \* \*

*Ours is a world of crucifixion.* We are all victims of a larger culture of death, and it is the same culture of death that deemed Jesus too dangerous to keep alive nearly 2,000 years ago on this night. We all come to this table this evening to remember the last meal of a convicted criminal who was executed the next morning. Jesus did not ask for food ordered out, but he sat down for a simple meal of bread and wine.

Jesus sat with his friends knowing that he would be betrayed, knowing that he would be executed, and probably knowing that everyone around him would commit suicide or be executed for being associated with him. Everything around him was dismembering and falling apart, and within hours he would be arrested, beaten, whipped, mocked, publicly belittled, and finally killed. The disciples were all marked by death for him, and even as they denied him, their own fate would be more firmly sealed by the cross at Gethsemane.

We should recall that Christians have always believed that the world was created by God through Jesus, the "first-begotten" or "only-begotten son," and that the sacrifice of Jesus was an essential culmination of God's plan for creation from the beginning of time, that God's salvation for us was part of a cosmic plan right from the beginning. It is important for us to remember that if this is the case, the crucifixion of Christ is also marked upon everything around us; the mark of Christ's death *is* all around us. All of creation has been waiting for the moment of crucifixion, the moment when God bled everything out that he had for us.

So it makes sense that Jesus took two very simple foods, bread and wine, found in any home, and said, when you eat this, you eat me, because even with simple food products made by human hands, because they exist, they are signs of the cross. And everything we eat, touch, or make has the sign of the cross upon them. Before this point in history, crucifixion was unknown, and when Jesus sat at table, the disciples were confused and amazed because they did not understand.

Our table features simple foods, bread and wine. The bread is probably different than the bread Jesus touched, and the wine is probably a little different. Nevertheless, they still bear the mark of Christ because they exist and are a part of our world. We come to this table as a people who are victims of a culture of death, and as a privileged people who are also participants and complicit with this culture of death. When we eat the crucifixion we pray that the crucifixion comes to us not only as culture or individuals breaking us down, but as a crucifixion from the inside out—that we carry ourselves as Jesus did, knowing that the unfolding of God into history is greater than ourselves; we carry our own cross with courage and grace; and that we reflect that grace in our discernment and criticism of the world and people around us.

This is how we come to this table on this night, along with other Christians around the world. We are a gathering of sinners tonight who remembers the last meal of a criminal on death row 2,000 years ago.

## Some Gods Must Die[1]
(Easter Vigil)
*Genesis 22:1–14; Revelation 21:22–27*

A significant question of the modern religious man or woman is how is it that people can claim to believe in God and fly planes into buildings? How can people claim to believe in a single God and enforce everyone to believe exactly the same way that I do? How is it that one can claim that God hates people, or wants them killed, for worshiping another God or worshiping the same God differently?

The idea of monotheism, the idea that there is one God, actually developed in the history of the world as a way of promoting diversity, because it would be foolish to believe that a single God must express itself exactly the same way for everybody everywhere. Having one God was politically expedient because it would allow for a religiously and culturally diverse nation, or empire, to believe that they worship the same God and to stop fighting each other over whose God is more powerful. Monotheism was politically expedient because a nation or empire could focus upon foreign military threats instead of internal religious conflicts if everyone worshiped the same god. In fact, if we take the history of religions seriously we would discover that the political nature of monotheism has been deeply influential upon Western society through its use in ancient Persia, Egypt, and Israel. Absolute Monotheism, the idea that there is only one single God in the universe, as an intellectual experiment, is not as old as Judaism, and it is not as old as our story of Abraham and Isaac. That is to say, the idea that there is only one single god, in the way that we think of this concept today, had not yet been developed at the time of the composition of the story of Abraham. (*In fact, I'll add as an aside, the idea of monotheism is not nearly as old as the Old Testament!*)

The typical Christian reading of this story is that it encapsulates trust in the divine, especially through and in spite of the absurd; I affirm this interpretation. The great Danish philosopher Søren Kierkegaard based his entire system of religious thought on this teaching of trust in the story of Abraham and Isaac. But more radically, Kierkegaard's understanding of this divine trust was that to trust God is the great leap of faith from the certain into the uncertain, from a God of hard evidence into a God of "perhaps" or "maybe": that faith based in certainty is foolishness, and embracing the grey areas of uncertainty is to step off of a cliff, knowing that God may not be there to catch you, but yet having the foolish faith to believe in it anyway.[1]

Let us take some time to read this text, Genesis 22:1–14, closely.

*After these things God tested Abraham. He said to him, "Abraham!" And he said, "Here I am."* (Gen. 22:1, NRSV as follows)

The "God" described in verse 1 in Hebrew is *Elohim*. Elohim is the same name that is used whenever Gods is used in the plural, such as in the First Commandment, "you shall not have any *Gods* before me." Abraham's "Here I am" is a very common response to God's call.

*He said, "Take your son, your only son Isaac, whom you love, and go to the land of Moriah, and offer him there as a burnt offering on one of the mountains that I shall show you."* (22:2)

In verse 2, Abraham is instructed to go "to the Land of Moriah." Where was this exactly? We know that Solomon's temple would be later built in Moriah, but we also know that there probably would have been a Semitic priest in Jerusalem, or what was believed to be Jerusalem during this time.

"Moriah" is really a range of mountains rather than a single one and would have been in the region of what is today Jerusalem, specifically near the seat of the eye of Moloch, described in the book of 2 Chronicles, as the valley of Gehenna, or the valley of Hell. This is exactly where the valley of Kidron meets the foot of what is today the city of Jerusalem, where Jesus would have entered the city on Palm Sunday, which at that time would have been the trash dump of the city. Prior to Jerusalem's settlement, this valley was a very holy site for the Canaanites; namely, it was where the God Moloch demanded a sacrifice of the firstborn children. (It was common back then to make former holy sites of a prior religion into a trash dump, which is what the Christians did to the site of the Temple in Jerusalem, before Mohammed came and reclaimed it for the Muslims later.)

My point is that *this* Elohim instructs Abraham to go into the range of mountains of Moriah and to sacrifice his first and only born son. This is a God appealing to an older tradition, which demanded that all parents sacrifice their first-born children for the God Moloch, who would burn their children to death, which is, again, described in several places elsewhere in the Bible.

> *Then Abraham said to his young men, "Stay here with the donkey; the boy and I will go over there; we will worship, and then we will come back to you." Abraham took the wood of the burnt offering and laid it on his son Isaac, and he himself carried the fire and the knife. So the two of them walked on together.* (22:5–6)

Reading verses 5 and 6, one might ask, who were the people in Abraham's entourage who kind of knew what was going on? We typically read this story as if Abraham's crew did not know what was happening, because this story is, at least on face value, crazy. But if these were men who knew the region, and knew its religious history, they surely knew what was about to happen, and it is clear that Abraham is the one who must offer the sacrifice of the child, because that is what was done in the style of worshiping the God Moloch. But the scripture states that he had "young men" with him; they, like Isaac, are not knowledgeable of the old gods and their traditions. Isaac is clearly not in the know, probably because he is unaware of the old ways.

Why is Abraham carrying a knife in verse 6? Abraham is going to kill Isaac as an act of mercy while setting him on fire. The point is not just a blood offering, but that Isaac's body will become a burned offering to the God who is demanding violence. In v. 6 it says Abraham is carrying the knife and the fire.

> *Isaac said to his father Abraham, "Father!" And he said, "Here I am, my son." He said, "The fire and the wood are here, but where is the lamb for a burnt offering?" Abraham said, "God himself will provide the lamb for a burnt offering, my son." So the two of them walked on together.* (22:7–8)

Again, Isaac doesn't know what is going on, but Abraham says that God will provide the lamb for the burned offering. Again, the word used for God here in Hebrew is "Elohim." We know how this goes. Abraham is about to kill Isaac, and then he is interrupted by the angel.

> *Then Abraham reached out his hand and took the knife to kill his son. But the angel of the Lord called to him from heaven, and said, "Abraham, Abraham!" And he said, "Here I am."* (22:10–11)

The name of God here changes. "The angel of the Lord." Not "God," Elohim, but "Lord," Yahweh. That's why the word "LORD" is in all caps in most translations of the Bible, to indicate a change of terminology here.

There is a slight change in expectation of sacrifice in the story. Abraham tells Isaac that the Elohim God will provide a lamb, which is a younger sheep that is not sexually active, and in the end a ram, which is a male, sexually active sheep is offered by the God Yahweh. A ram is used for breeding, where a lamb's value is usually to eat, since the meat of a younger sheep is more desirable than mutton, the meat of an older sheep or a ram.

What I am suggesting here is that this story is, on one hand, a story of trust, but it is also a story of temptation. Abraham was so fixated on the one God, and believing what that one God appeared to be saying, that he realized that a false God, or a God from the past, demanded violence of him, demanded a human sacrifice.

So often we see things that we think are good news for our faith, or "wins" for the Christian faith when they really are false gods speaking to us, and we're not able to take a step back from our own limited experiences, or what we think we're hearing, that we simply obey out of obedience. The reality is that gods in which we should not believe, gods that should be long dead, are speaking to us from the grave, and we give them substance by following them.

The past months we have seen Christians celebrating the U.S. Supreme Court decisions involving employer's rights to control employees' sexual and women's health. We all know this is a bad move for the religious freedom of everyone. The irony is that this is not a win for religious liberty, but a win for certain religious individuals who wish to impose their own views on others, especially those making minimum wage or close to it, the working poor. The very next day the same companies petitioned the president calling themselves victims for not being allowed to receive federal funding because of their victimizing hiring policies. It is all a big circle of being victimizer and victim in the same breath.

Few of us, too few of us, stand back and ask, "Is this really what Christianity is about?" Would Christians be celebrating these acts in the same way if it were Muslim companies wishing to apply Sharia Law in ways that violate discrimination and health care compensation? The entire situation appears as a subconscious admission that there are in fact many gods, and whichever god directly benefits me right now, in this moment, is the one who is to be worshiped. By believing in one god, and demanding that everyone believe and practice faith in exactly the same way, we see emerging a *pantheon of paganisms*, where gods are connected to certain territories, to certain businesses or trades, who at any given time are theologically designed to serve *me* in the *now,* and then move on to the next god whenever it is convenient or financially expedient.

The God of Moses, who calls himself "Yahweh"—the sound of wind, the sound of breath—is the same God who halts the system of sacrifice, interrupting the system of victimizers victimizing victims. This God does not demand blood, does not demand violence, but instead asks us to follow the sacrificial animal, to live self-sacrificially, to apply ourselves as *living* sacrifice, rather than a *burned* sacrifice, or not living in a system where my giving sacrifices of other beings justifies or atones for whatever I say or do.

This God declares boldly to us: "Those other gods are dead." But we so often resurrect those Gods of blood and sacrifice and use the name of the true God to justify our wants and desires. Those are false Gods who must die for the true God to live with us. We can prop up the false Gods with our money, with our "rights," with our politics, with our elevation of ideas, with our weapons, with our addictions to ourselves or our drugs, to our culture, to our desire not to offend others, to our obsession with living in a state of war or violence. We worship the Satan of this great multitude of Gods with the love of ourselves, and not with the path of genuine sacrifice.

* * *

In Revelation 21, Jesus, at the end of time, is expressed as the great sacrificial animal, the God who leads us away from sacrificing each other, by leading the example of sacrificing itself. There will be then no churches, no streets with names, no more nations, no more flags, no more armies, no more independence days, for it is all one great Sabbath. There is only the Lamb. No abomination. No falsehood. The only truth is the sacrifice of God, and whether we followed suit with that sacrifice.

Abraham's leap of faith was not just to place his son on the altar as a burned sacrifice, but rather to stop the sacrifice and to trust that it isn't that God changed his mind, but that the true God does not demand blood sacrifice. There can be no justification for human blood any longer, and any God or religious system that believes otherwise is an elaborate way of worshiping false Gods or ourselves, which is to say, worshiping Satan. The question for us is whether we are really ready to enter that place of peace or to continue the killing, or supporting the apparatuses which continue the violence, to stop worshiping ourselves? To come to the altar with nothing in our hands, and simply surrender ourselves for the sake of humanity, as a means of following the God whose blood sacrifice ends all other sacrifice? Understanding that the sacrifice of God in Jesus on the altar of the cross is not just a blood offering to a dead God for the sake of humanity, *but an invitation* where we choose the path of sacrificing ourselves for the sake of the greater hope for peace, the hope of the lamb.

## I Believe in the Insurrection![1]
(Easter Sunday)
*1 Corinthians 12:1–3, Luke 24:1–43*

I grew up in a church that placed a high priority on the notion that the events of the first Easter Sunday are historically accurate, and the truth of Easter is historically accurate. I was also always taught that if one denies the resurrection one denies the Bible as a sound historical document. The problem with this kind of thinking is, however, that when we think this way we exclude those from the conversation who want to ask the tough questions about Easter, and exclude those who struggle with their faith.

The traditional belief is that we get special privileges for believing that the resurrection of Jesus is a historical event, namely, that if we believe in the Gospels as facts, we will be rewarded and we'll go to heaven. It's all very simple. And it would seem that Christianity through history really is that simple: Christianity has not on the whole led to the cessation of war, or poverty. Christians in our country were behind the end of slavery, but it was also the Christians who were very much for slavery. Christians have always used their beliefs and the fact that we believe that we are religiously and historically superior because of the special privileges that we get for believing to deny the civil rights and liberties of others, and to perpetuate mechanisms of injustice and the mechanisms of intolerance, and to justify war.

Many Christians are quite offended by anyone reminding us of this history, so we go to great lengths to revise the history and forget. But the facts remain, and the hypocrisy is this: *If Christianity is simply a faith that makes a statement of history, we need to own the scandal of our own history,* and along with this history, its long tradition of failure.

If we are to parade the resurrection of Jesus from the dead as Good News, we need to recognize that for the world that has been colonized under Christian history; and to the Jews who have suffered holocausts (and I use the word holocaust here as a plural word) under our history;

and the Native Americans who have been lied to by Christians often waving a flag of peace; and to the peoples we have exploited time and time again over some sense of religion with a sense of cultural superiority that our historical insistence regarding the resurrection of Jesus is Bad News. In fact, it is *very Bad News* for many.

I propose that we reclaim the Good News, and rethink what it means to believe in the resurrection of Jesus. St. Paul's instructions in his first letter to the Corinthians offer us some clues. St. Paul says that only from the Holy Spirit may we say that "Jesus is Lord." As we proclaim the resurrection of Christ in our worship, then, we may only say it genuinely if it is to be stated from our mouths when filled with the Holy Spirit. To say "Jesus is Lord" and then enact hatred, bigotry, or war on someone else is to curse God—and I am suggesting then that much of the last 2,000 years of Christian history was in fact not Christian history but the worst kind of heresy. It was Christianity posing as Christianity. It was the opposite of Christianity.

If we can accept that the Christ handed down to us through the terrible history of Christianity, as justified by the fact of the resurrection, is probably not the best way to think about the resurrected Christ, we are empowered today not to sit back passively in our pews and just accept as Gospel as an easily-digestible sermon. Instead, the Good News that I have to preach to you today is that the Word of God is *empowering* and *enacting* something New, something *completely New,* into you all as individuals and more importantly into us as a church in this hour of worship on the most important holy day of this year.

The resurrection is not an excuse for those of us who are generally part of the middle class of the dominant race in this country to pat ourselves on the back for believing in something written in a dead language in a book thousands of years ago. The resurrection does not make us better than other people who do not believe in the resurrection, but instead the resurrection challenges us to *provoke* the Holy Spirit to *fill our mouths* and *enflesh into our bodies,* so that in proclaiming the Good News of Easter the Gospel is a Good News to the poor, the lonely, the dying, the weak, those who are being crucified by principalities and powers and spiritual wickedness in high places even as we gather together today.

The resurrection does not call us into surrendering our thinking brains at the door, into believing something absolutely fantastical, but instead it challenges us to subvert and rebel radically against the culture in which we live, this culture where so much of what we do does not matter in any ultimate sense, a culture that teaches children to kill each other, and a culture that allows adults to exploit and abuse each other in our actions. Too often for too many people Easter is the day of the year that we come to church to have our class and privilege reified, that we proclaim that we believe in something the rest of the world does not, and this is why we have the leisure to gather together for pretty music and easy religion.

Instead, Easter *invites us into the spiritual location of the crucifixion and resurrection.* In other words, Easter is the location of the reality of the world—and by reality I mean the worst, grimiest, and harshest aspects of reality. If Easter invites us into the location of the resurrection, we are like the women who are speaking so fantastically about what has happened on the first Easter that the disciples are completely confused. Easter is what challenges us to do radical acts of kindness that make absolutely no sense, Easter invites us to sacrifice ourselves beyond what is convenient and beyond what is tax-deductible.

Easter offers us the *courage to act* and the *courage to proclaim loudly* the Good News to the point that those in powerful positions in the dominant religion (which we have already established as not being really rooted in God) and those in the dominant powers of government become scared of what we represent and do as Christians. We should remember that the disciples didn't just set up shop and build large church buildings and move on from there, they were all gruesomely killed. Those with religious and political power executed not just some of them, but all of them. Easter was Good News for them, but it wasn't about giving some nostalgia for old times, or singing the old hymns that support old ways of thinking about God, nor was it simply a day off work, but the first Easter was instead the beginning of a revolution that was so dangerous that they were marked for death the moment Jesus broke bread with them. They could not sing of old ways of thinking about God, because the risen Christ represents something new.

\* \* \*

It is the risen Christ who, when the disciples were just calming down from their disbelief, asks them if he has any food. So stunned, they gave the risen Christ leftovers to eat—keep in mind this was before refrigeration. This story reminds me a little of when you're sick, you finally know you're coming back to your old self when you get your appetite back. For the disciples, Jesus wasn't really "back" in any real sense until he eats their old leftover food. And it was eating some leftover food that they finally believed, and then accepted their individual and communal roles in history. They too had to follow Christ and preach the risen Christ—and the preaching of the risen Christ was not a message necessarily of comfort for most people, it was one that *radically reversed* the social scheme.

So even against all odds of the resurrection of Christ being real, I boldly proclaim that Easter is a *reversal* of what we typically think about the resurrection—that we authentically return to the risen Christ, the *Biblical Christ,* who truly is Good News for the poor and the downtrodden. In proclaiming a faith in the resurrection I then preach to you this morning the Good News of *the insurrection,* that our response to the resurrection not be one that continues history into the banal nothingness of the *status quo* and what we have come to expect from ourselves and others, but that our belief in Easter be a belief in new life, and new hope, and that life matters in the here-and-now. Easter is decidedly the opposite of anything that enacts injustice or intolerance, or war or hatred. Our practice of Easter is to begin to be the building blocks of a Kingdom that hopes for more, and reflects a belief in God that is generous, hospitable, loving, and accepting.

\* \* \*

Now we can go home from this place of worship unchanged, having fulfilled our family and social obligations to attend church on Easter. Or we can begin the hard and tragic work of continuing the resurrection, that is, the *insurrected resurrection,* by sitting down together not to a grand meal, as the meal awaiting many of us at home is, but a simple meal of bread and wine. We partake in the body and blood so that *we now become the body and blood,* and with the risen flesh of Christ, we invoke again the presence of Christ as on the first Easter.

If the Christ we meet today is the same Christ we've always greeted on Easter Sunday every year, where we are only compelled to go home and eat our ham without fundamentally changing our lives, it's now time for us to return back to the Jesus we meet in the Bible, an actually New Christ, and sit down for leftovers. Again, it's telling that the first disciples recognized Jesus by their food. If you have ever taken communion and thought that the bread was stale, think of it this way—the meal where the disciples finally recognized Jesus was one where Jesus ate stale, leftover food while the disciples were too excited to figure out what to do next.

In taking the bread and wine today, on this Easter Sunday that follows the crucifixion, descent into Hell, and resurrection of Christ, along with the horror of Christian history that is handed down to us, we sit at the table with a Christ present to us in our stale food, the same Christ who ate before the amazed disciples, and inspired them to begin a revolution and rebellion against the religious and political powers of their world. The mandate of Easter is now on us, because we know that every time I pass someone along the side of the road who is in need of help *we deny the resurrection.* And every time I remain silent for those who have no voice, *we deny the resurrection.* Every time we place my so-called "civil rights" over the well-being and safety of others, and every time we prevent those who are of other races, classes, nationalities, and orientations different than me from sharing in the privileges we have, *we deny the resurrection.*[2] Every time I fail to practice Easter, by saying with thin words and empty gestures, "I believe in the resurrection," or affirm that "He is risen, indeed" without a commitment to make this world a better place, we, along with the horror of history, boldly proclaim that we deny the resurrection.

So the question I leave with you in this Easter sermon is not whether you believe in the resurrection, but rather this: Will you respond to this new Easter, this Easter that is today, by going home and allowing this to be one more Easter that follows a long line of Easters that represent the trajectory of the downward spiral of the history of Christendom? Or is this Easter a New Easter, a New Day, a New season, a New moment in history where we as individuals and as a community make a tremendous announcement that the culture of death in which we live is "on notice," because we leave from this church as New Flesh of the Resurrection, empowered and ready to build a culture of life everywhere we go?

\* \* \*

In answering this question, I share an African parable. Everyone in a small town would line up to ask this wise old man, a sage, their deepest and most difficult questions. The older the man got, the more respect he gained from his community and the more his reputation spread, the line to speak with him always seemed to be longer and longer.

One young man decided that he wanted to find a way to trick the old man, so he came up with a plan. He waited in line for hours to speak with him.

When it was finally his turn the young man said to the sage, "I hold behind my back in each of my hands two baby chicks. If you are so wise, why don't you tell me whether the baby chicks in my hands alive or dead? If you answer correctly, I will recognize your wisdom and your reputation will spread even beyond what it already has. But if you answer incorrectly, I have finally proven that you are truly not wise."

The old man thought about this for a few seconds and replied, "You must think I am a fool! I know that you have those chicks alive in your hands, ready to squeeze the life out of them if I say that they are alive, to show me two dead chicks. But if I tell you they are dead, you will spare them both and reveal them to be alive. And if I say one is dead and one is alive, you will simply do the opposite!"

The crowd around them was astonished, and the young man walked away, discouraged that he had been publicly exposed as having attempted to defraud the wise man.

But the wise men advised the crowd: "Do not judge that young man, for his youth is to blame for his resentment of me. But there is a deeper truth in this lesson for you to discover." And the wise man began to walk away.

The crowd began to chatter, asking, "What is the truth that we are to learn? Not to challenge your wisdom?"

The wise man turned around and said, "The lesson is that *the truth is always in your hands.*"[3]

*This is the truth of Easter: The truth is not in the Bible.* Neither is the truth found in the empty words of creeds or proclamations of faith. *The truth is in your hands.*

## Open Hearts, Open Minds, Rigor Mortis
(Easter 6)
*Isaiah 45:1–6; Acts 16:9–15*

The conversion of Lydia in Acts 16 is a rather obscure story in the Bible because at first glance it does not seem to be an extraordinary story, unless we pick apart the details and symbolism of the story. To recount, St. Paul, with little success in preaching in Asia Minor, travels into Europe following a vision that God was calling him to preach the Gospel there. One interesting note in the story is that the narrator, who was probably Luke, refers to himself and St. Paul as "we" traveling from Samothrace, Neapolis (today known as Kavala), and then to Philippi, which was then, the Bible says, "the leading district of Macedonia." These cities are all now known as part of modern-day Greece.

We should remember that during this time this entire region, although it had its own history, culture, and language, was colonized as part of the Roman Empire. Paul and Luke could travel freely within its boundaries because the districts that used to be their own states or kingdoms were now swallowed up into the Empire of Rome. What Paul and Luke had in common with these other folks, who would have been understood as being from different races and different cultures, is that they were *all* oppressed citizens of the political and economic machine of the Roman Empire, although the kind of oppression that the different regions experienced was sometimes quite different from region to region.

At the same time, we should recognize that when the Holy Spirit commands Paul to cross some borders within the Empire, a few short boat rides take him and his cohort of disciples into another continent, and in this passage of scripture we witness Christianity crossing into Europe for the first time. The journey may be somewhat short, but geographically, this is a transitional moment, which represents the entrance of the Christian faith into a new continent—a continent that is not only home to the oppressive Empire in Rome, but a large continent of religions and cultures largely unknown to Paul and the disciples. Europe was a largely strange and unfamiliar place to them.

According to the Book of Acts, Luke and Paul arrive to Philippi on the Sabbath, and they're looking for some other Jews to pray with, and they assume that there would be Jews present. While searching for Jews, they meet a woman named Lydia. Tradition teaches that Lydia was a Jew who found herself in Philippi, but there is really no evidence that Lydia was a Jew, even though Luke calls her "a worshipper of God." We don't know if she was Jewish or whether she was of some other religion, but Luke recognized her immediately as a worshipper of the same God.

Lydia is described as being from "the city of Thyatira" and is a merchant of purple cloth. She eagerly listened to what Paul and Luke told her about Jesus, and she has her entire household baptized. She then invited them to stay at their home.

I question the historical account of this story on the grounds of the name of this woman—"Lydia"—and that she was from "Thyatira." The word "Lydia" literally means "someone from Lydia." Lydia was, hundreds of years before this time, its own country, its own kingdom, that existed as the Arzawa Empire, which lasted from the fifteenth to the fourteenth centuries BCE, and later the Lydian Empire, from 1200 to 546 BCE—the latter year of 546 being the date the fall of the Lydian empire is important, dating closely to return of the Jews from their exile in Babylon, which I'll return to in a moment. If you know your geography, we started our story out with Paul leaving what is today Turkey for what is today Greece: where he was leaving, and where he had no success preaching was in Western Turkey, which would have been previously known as what was the Lydian Empire.

The Bible refers to Lydia as being from Thyatira. Thyatira is the Lydian name of what is today the Turkish city of Akishar; the word "Thyatira" means "daughter" and was known to be a commercial center for dyeing textiles and the trading of indigo. So it seems to me that this character named Lydia of Thyatira is symbolic of someone from the old Lydian empire in Asia Minor, the place where Paul was unable to preach before.

Lydia is interesting because she is the first convert in Europe, but as the first convert in Europe, first of all, she is obviously female, and she is a merchant with some economic means, which was unusual. She was also culturally displaced from her home and living in Philippi. What she had in common with the Philippians she lived among was that she was also a subject of a foreign emperor, whose reign gives her the ability to live where she is living but she also continues to live under oppression, no matter where she goes within the Empire, and as a merchant who has a house and a business she surely paid her taxes to the Emperor. She was still middle-class, compared to Paul, but like Paul and everyone else, she was still lives under the tyranny of the Empire.

As a symbol of this region of Lydia, this character named Lydia represents an entire culture whose history goes back as far as the Jewish people. The Lydian Empire, however, ended with a bang, and the legacy of the end of the Lydian Empire would be influential on the region for years. The final king of Lydia was Croesus, from where you may have heard the expression that someone is "as rich as Croesus." Croesus lived from 595 to 547 BCE, and was known to be the first king to issue coinage backed by gold, and some coins were even put into circulation by the king that were made of gold.

King Croesus inherited the throne from his father, King Alyattes of Lydia, who died in 560. When Croesus became King, he found himself the ruler of a small empire whose borders were increasingly dangerous. To the west were the Greeks, who were becoming increasingly hostile to the Lydians, but more importantly, the Persian Empire's influence in the region made it increasingly clear that it was just a matter of time before the Persians would force Croesus out of power.

King Croesus went into modern-day Greece, to Delphi, to the sanctuary of the god Apollo, where the King asked whether he should wage war or seek an alliance with the Persians. There the Oracle of Delphi (speaking as the god Apollo) famously proclaimed to him that if he would attack the Persians, he would destroy a great empire. Following this advice, Croesus made an alliance with the Spartans and began a war against King Cyrus of the Persian Empire in 547. Croesus captured the Persian city of Pteria and made all of the city's inhabitants slaves. King Cyrus responded, forcing the Lydians out of Pteria and back into the Lydian capital city of Sardis.

King Cyrus sent just under 50,000 soldiers into the capital city in December of 547, and there met Croesus' forces of 105,000 men, which included Arabian, Babylonian, and Egyptian mercenaries. The Persians took the Lydians by surprise, and even though the Persians were outnumbered two-to-one in a foreign capital city, the Lydian casualties were heavy, and King Croesus and his family were captured. While the details of his death are not clear, historians believe that King Cyrus of Persia ordered that King Croesus and his family to be burned alive on a funeral pyre.

Legend is that while King Croesus was burning, he prayed to the god Apollo, remembering that the oracle told him that if he attacked the Persians he would destroy an empire: the empire that was destroyed was not the Persian Empire, but his own Kingdom of Lydia. The death of Croesus marked the end of Lydia as a sovereign political state.

To review: King Cyrus ordered the execution of King Croesus of Lydia, this same King Cyrus who was celebrated as the righteous king in the Old Testament who released the Jews from their exile in Babylon and allowed them to return home to Jerusalem. The Jews celebrated Cyrus as a righteous King, and some Jews even regarded this Persian King as the messiah, and there are remnants of this in the Old Testament books of Ezra[1] and in Isaiah, which we read from this morning.

Jews regarded King Cyrus as a savior, but the Lydians regarded Cyrus as a destroyer. After Lydia became part of the Persian Empire, the region changed hands several times. Alexander the Great of Macedonia acquired Lydia though Alexander's great conquests; when Alexander died and his empire ended, Lydia became part of the Seleucid Empire, and later changed hands into the Kingdom of Pergamum. When Pergamum's last king, Attalus III, died without an heir, to avoid war he left the entire Kingdom to the Roman Empire.

Now I know these countries and names of kings might be obscure to many of you, but the point of this is that Lydia was a region that had completely lost its identity, completely lost its name, and to modern readers of the Bible, when we encounter a woman named Lydia, we no longer realize the symbolic or political significance of this character.

The character "Lydia of Thyatira," then, is representative of *someone completely displaced*. She is living not too far from where she is from, but living in a different continent separates her significantly from the culture of her origin. She is a woman with commercial interests, a female merchant who is middle class. Her country was destroyed by the same King who freed the Jews from their exile; the same ruler, King Cyrus, who burned her king alive is regarded as a messiah or savior of the people of Saint Paul.

But when Lydia meets Paul, she is found inquisitive and reverent, and her *heart was open*. This is the most important piece of the story: for an audience that would have known her backstory, and understood that this was a woman who somehow immigrated to another place, and found success in another culture, and was successful through the trade of dyeing fabric, she had every excuse to no longer find reverence or religion in the old gods of her own people. Yet she is discovered worshiping God—how she had knowledge of God we do not know—and with an *open heart*, accepts Jesus as her savior, and her whole household is baptized, and she extends hospitality to the traveling disciples. Her heart was *open*.

You can tell when you are talking to someone or teaching someone whether they are teachable or not. We know that this goes the same way with religion and in the church. We all know people who think that if the church music, or the flowers, or the way the minister dresses isn't exactly what they think the church should be, it's not the church. And surrounding those folks with closed hearts, religious communities develop around the concept that what we always do in church must be the old ways, a celebration of the past, at all cost: even forsaking the truth or even the future of the church. It did not matter who picked the songs out or what the songs were, the fact is that anything that smells like change is regarded as negative. When we close our hearts, our hearts are hardened. I call it *rigor mortis.*

But when we learn with an *open heart,* when we listen with an open heart, when we offer and receive hospitality with an open heart, when we worship with an open heart, the Holy Spirit brings us into new and unexpected territories. Paul was facing failure in his preaching in Asia Minor, and the Spirit provoked him to go into Europe. And there he met this character, Lydia, who was already converted before she even really met Paul and Luke. The Holy Spirit worked with them out of failure, and ordered them to go into new places and to meet unexpected people.

Lydia had every reason to have a closed heart, like many people in our industrialized society, she had enough wealth that she knew she had a meal coming to her, she wasn't struggling. For industrialized or secular people, God or gods are not needed to supply our "daily bread"—that's what money is for in industrialized societies; we place our faith in money rather than God. We can pray, "give us this daily bread," but we know our next meal is not coming from God, but from our money. Lydia was wealthy enough to not hope for her next meal, yet she is found by Paul to be worshiping the true God. Lydia believed in the Gospel before she met Paul; Paul simply filled in the blanks in her spiritual knowledge. She had an open heart.

We all have parts of our hearts that are hardened. We all have our own fundamentalisms. The Holy Spirit provokes us out of these stiff entrenchments; the Spirit calls us to not be a mighty fortress but to be *plastic,* accepting, forgiving, representatives of the weaknesses of God. We all have back-histories: we've been to jail, we've done things of which we are not proud, we have participated in the racism and sexism in the world. None of us are innocent.

But if our hearts are opened, we expose ourselves, we humble ourselves to each other and to God in new ways that will demand a new way of discipleship. And it is on this point that we can talk about Christians who "talk the talk" and Christians who "walk the walk." When we talk about preachers or people to "talk the talk" and "walk the walk" very often the implication is that our beliefs and actions don't seem to match. I'm more interested in whether we walk with an openness, and whether we talk with an openness that allows for something new to happen, and allows for someone new to come into the sanctuary, and an openness whether the Holy Spirit can blow a new breeze into our open windows.

We can wear jewelry with an open heart on it, and put it on display for everyone to see. We even can hang relics of having an open heart exquisitely on a corpse. We can put the words "open hearts" on our church sign, like the Methodists have ("Open hearts, open minds, open doors"), but if we don't practice an openness to the Holy Spirit, we are not only limiting the future of the church, but we place new limitations and idolatries upon what we mean by the word God.

To conclude, to go back to the question of what it meant that Paul and Luke found Lydia "worshiping God," I believe that it is an important, if not largely lost and unknown, spiritual practice of Christianity to *have an open heart*. Just being open to the Holy Spirit, and being open to the newness of God working around us in the present, is a worship practice. We signify this when we welcome new members into this church, we will again ritually welcome new members into this church again in a few weeks. All churches say they want to grow, but it is a worship of the Holy Spirit to make this growth and be open to this growth to be a spiritual practice. *This* is now our task.

# Pentecost and the Season after Pentecost

## A History of Missing the Big Point: Is 160 Years Enough?
(Pentecost)
*John 14:8–17, Acts 2:1–21, Psalm 104*

On this day, some 2,000 years ago, the Holy Spirit descended down onto the first Christians, which for them at the time reminded them all that Jesus said he would send the Spirit to them. So Jesus returns to the heavens in the Ascension, and in the absence of Christ in the world, a new era begins on the day of Pentecost. The Pentecost places authority and blessing upon the church as the new institution to continue the work of Jesus in his physical absence. But the absence of Jesus is not as simple as Jesus just disappearing, since we remember that Jesus says that the Kingdom of God is *among you*.

And ever since then, the presence of God in the world is to be understood as acting through the community of those gathered in Jesus' name, that is, the church. So often we do not take seriously enough what is really being said in this story, namely, that *we are the presence of God in the world.* The function of the church is to enact God in this world. To build the Kingdom. To reverse the social order. To preach God's justice in grace, mercy, and charity. For so many the church is an optional element of the Christian life—being part of the church is not simply to support a building in a neighborhood or to support a pastor; Christianity is not a spectator sport. Being part of the church is doing the hard work, though giving, through volunteering, through self-sacrificial acts, for the community.

So when Jesus says that the Kingdom of God is *among you,* I am one of those people who thinks Jesus meant what he said. He is speaking both metaphorically and when he says the Kingdom of God is *among you.* By speaking in metaphors, Jesus is saying that when we believe that we are created in God's image, it is not that we physically *look* like God, but that we have a little piece of God in us as his children—in other words, we're from the same stock as God, we're made in God's image, which is why

Jesus comes to us as a human being and not some other animal, as Jesus is a brother to us.

What Jesus means, quite literally, when he says that the Kingdom of God is in you is that you and I together are the bearers of the Holy in the present world. So often when things go our way, we ask why God didn't swoop down out of heaven to stop something bad from happening, or we ask why God allows bad things to happen to us: *Why do bad things happen to good people?* The fact is that if life was a constant pleasant vacation it wouldn't be life, and we often assume that we are getting punished for bad things happening in life, when we forget just how human life is. But we should remember that God, as Jesus, did not have a perfect life—he was born into poverty, was a refugee for at least some of his childhood, was likely homeless for his last years and died the death of a criminal executed by the state. It seems to me that God's life on earth didn't go so well, either, given his state execution.

When Jesus says that the Kingdom of God is in us, the impetus is now upon us to make God known in a more welcomed and welcoming way than what Jesus experienced during his lifetime. It's worth mentioning that one of the primary symbols of Pentecost, the tongue loosened with the Spirit, is the opposite of the tongues Jesus encountered in the world. People around Jesus were not willing to speak radically against injustice, and like today religious leaders were very careful about the words they used so as not to irritate the politicians, and people were certainly not willing to speak up against the persecution of Jesus. If we can think of a closed mouth opening, and opening to speak the Good News, this is our first image of Pentecost.

Another symbol that is getting reversed here in Pentecost is the fire. Fire is always changing; you need fire to keep warm and you need to be careful with fire. Fire is the opposite of religion that is cold, always says "no," and is more concerned with keeping the laws and maintaining the social order than serving God. Fire suggests to us a God who thirsts for change in our institutions, our ways of life, and in our personal ways of thinking. Once we catch fire we can have the fire put out or we can let it consume us—God wants us to be consumed by the fire of Pentecost, because the small spark of the divine, the Kingdom of God, is already inside of us, yearning to blaze as a social reality in the world!

The third symbol of Pentecost that is a symbol of reversal is the dove. The dove is a symbol of peace, forgiveness, and reconciliation, but it's also a symbol of freedom and liberation. When the Holy Spirit comes down upon the church like a dove, the dove is a free bird—it goes where it chooses. Birds can be predictable and they can be unpredictable; but not just one or the other, birds are both predictable and unpredictable. So the Holy Spirit moves with us through seasons of the year, seasons of our lives; the Holy Spirit migrates towards us and away from us. The Dove is a symbol that is the opposite of a slow or restricted animal, it is a bird whose cage has disappeared, and the whole world is now the mission field. God is no longer to be understood as only a God of the Jews but a God of everyone.

These three symbols—the loosened tongue, fire, and the dove—are symbols of the church. But over the years we have observed that Christianity has lost its fire, the church has lost its radical message of liberating freedom from oppression, and Christians are often too busy meddling in politics or controversial issues rather than their own social holiness or sanctification. Or when we see Christians getting excited about causes it is often just for show or self-serving. This is such a problem for the church today that people on the outside understand this, even if we inside the church do not. The obsession that churches have with the politics of marriage, and abortion, and the unequivocal support of American empire, and limiting the rights of immigrants, the latter which the Bible says so much directly toward, is the opposite of Christianity. This is preaching that not only has little to do with the core message of the Gospel but it is a message that is directly working *against* the Holy Spirit: it limits the power of the voice of the loosened tongues of the Community of Christ. It worships the self, the state, the powers and principalities, which is to say, *it worships Satan*. It is the opposite of Christianity.

Yet, in our society, people are drawn to religion that preaches old-school values, even while the Jesus we meet in the Bible is far more interested in social justice and personal holiness, and his greatest command is to love in the radical way that he loves, and his promise is that the Holy Spirit will come to us. It would seem that we can see now how the horror of history has worked out, as we are blindly progressing into yet another war baited by propaganda and fear. It is easy to see how the history of the church is the history of missing the Big Point.

This time in which we live now, in this era of history *after* the first Pentecost, is one that should be marked by loosened tongues, fire, and the symbol of the liberated dove. Two thousand years later we still haven't figured this out, even while we wait for Jesus to return we need to acknowledge that we have not fully embraced the meaning of the Day of Pentecost. We need to ask whether we really are speaking with loosened tongues, whether we really are on fire for the Gospel, and whether our message is a genuine liberation—or whether the Christianity we preach and represent is the same old, tired religion that Jesus died to get us away from. Will the Kingdom of God be *in you,* or will you let the Kingdom of God die with the words of Jesus, written down in some old book? Does the Kingdom of God go with you or does it stay behind you in church, or do you just hope for it in the future? These are our questions today, and they are the same questions Jesus leaves us with.

* * *

Coming into our 160th anniversary in this church, we are at an important crossroads as a church. We know that this church has a bright future, but do we really believe it in a way that inspires our vision? Peter, addressing the first church service envisions the community of Christ as being one where the young will see visions, and the old will dream dreams. What is our vision? Is it one of more of the same? Is it a vision where we behave as if we are boldly prepared for the 1950s? Or is it one where we are ready to enact and be the change that the Gospel so fervently desires for us in this place, right now?

Are we ready to be sacrificial, and to take up our cross, to get there? I have always believed that the thing that holds back churches is a theology of scarcity: a belief that there is not enough to go around, a belief that the church is best served limited by its resources. This is how we and many churches operate, often facilitated by endowments and dead people's money. Those endowments in churches everywhere are disappearing, those same endowments that are the rock upon which so many churches rest.

The Good News for us is that we no longer have the luxury of putting faith in these endowments and trust funds. We are now being called to the line to see what stuff we are truly made of. *Are we ready to cross that boundary from a gospel of scarcity to a gospel of plenty?* Are we ready to take that step of deepest faith into uncharted territory? Are we ready to trust, and I mean really trust, that God will provide for us and for the church? And are we ready to believe what Jesus said, that we ourselves are the ones who facilitate and direct of how God moves in this world in this church?

Or, is it all a big lie? Is 160 years enough for this community of faith? Or 160 years, give or take a few?

\* \* \*

Pentecost was not just one day. In our church calendar, Pentecost is a season. The symbols of Pentecost are loosened tongues, fire, and the dove. But Pentecost is more than a season, in the Christian view of history Pentecost is the entire reality in which we live after the first Pentecost: *we must never forget this.* That we still live, and we are a church that is *Pentecostal,* we live in Pentecost times. Some Pentecostal churches speak in tongues and dance in the aisle, but our call today is to speak with loosened tongues, to be on fire with and for the Spirit, and to radically change and reverse course and move with the gushing of wind and like the flight patterns of doves. We as a church must search for a New Pentecost to revive us and gift us all with loosened tongues, the fire of the Gospel, and the liberation of a bird. We are blessed that God has called us into finding new directions, to reclaim the message of building the kingdom, speaking and practicing justice, and being found faithful.

The work of God's Kingdom is not to be found in politicians. When we blindly support politicians or the state, we are practicing an atheism that God is not present in the church. The work of God's Kingdom is not to be found in the theology of money, that we place our faith in a monetary number we all have attached to us that controls so much of what we do, and makes us never feel as if we have enough. The work of God's Kingdom is not to be found in ourselves and ourselves alone, because this is a selfish and self-serving religion. The work of God's Kingdom is to spawn out of this church, and practiced faithfully can branch out into enormous directions.

The Pentecost-like change that we all wish to bring about within our community needs to rekindle right here, inside of this church. It is not going to happen any other way. The bottom-line question, which we must all ask, is *whether 160 years is enough for this church, or do we believe that God is calling us into something new?* And this question is the question of whether we really believe in the God known to us as Father, Son, and Holy Spirit: Do we believe in this God of which Jesus speaks, this Kingdom of God, planted inside each one of us?

## Blessed Necromancy
(Proper 5)
*1 Kings 17:17–24; Luke 7:11–17*

Ever since I put this week's sermon title on the sign out front, people have been asking me, "what is *necromancy?*" Necromancy is a strange word for a fairly simple idea. Necromancy is the magical practice of raising the dead. Usually necromancy is a word attributed to the occult, and is often why we have popular images of pagans or witches hanging out in cemeteries. But at its definition, necromancy is plainly a part of the Christian faith—not just because we believe in Jesus, who raises from the dead, but because the Jesus tradition teaches that he raised people from the dead. So our scriptures today feature two stories of necromancy from the Bible, first of Elijah raising the dead, and the second where Jesus practices necromancy.

Our story of Jesus raising the widow's son from the dead, from the Gospel of Luke, is one of the handful of stories that only occurs only in the Gospel of Luke and not in the other Gospels in the Bible. Often scholars consider these stories to be of little value or not having much merit, because the fact they only occur in one place suggests that this may be a fabrication of the Jesus story. And these stories are not often told in church much because they're not seen as having much importance.

My perspective on these more obscure stories is that just because the story is only in one Gospel is not a reason to discount it, but to me the uniqueness of this story suggests that Luke is trying to make some kind of particular point that may not be made in other ways with the story.

The story opens with Jesus on the move, and comes to the village of Nain. There he and the disciples encounter a funeral procession, a dead person being taken from a home. Now this might not have been so memorable, except that the dead person is a young boy. I think we can all relate to this—we see obituaries in the paper every day, but when it is a child that died I think we tend to have a group response of empathy for the family. As distant observers, we often mourn the death of children in our community differently than older people, not only because of the broken potential that a death of a child represents, but also because the death of a child is an incomprehensible experience that even the suggestion of it startles us—especially if we have known someone who has gone through it. And unfortunately, most of us have had an experience within our own family or someone else's family of losing a child. We understand the community tragedy that resides in the death of a child. The Bible says that when Jesus saw the boy's mother, his heart broke.

Jesus then touches the child's coffin and the boy comes back to life and begins talking! Jesus then presented the boy to his mother.

\* \* \*

Most scholars agree that this story is an attempt by the author of the Gospel of Luke to recast the older Hebrew Bible narratives to the Jesus story, connecting Jesus to Elijah, who, in the book of 1 Kings, proved his worthiness as a prophet by raising a boy from the dead, by the power of God. But Luke's point in making this connection has a couple differences between Elijah and Jesus. In the story of Elijah, the prophet raises the dead boy as an act of atonement, to make right a wrong—the woman blamed Elijah for bringing bad things into her home. In the Jesus story, Jesus simply has empathy for the widow, and performs a miracle out of deep compassion for her. The woman did not do anything to deserve the miracle other than her situation emotionally affected Jesus.

Another difference between stories is that the scriptures go out of their way to indicate that Elijah is doing his miracle by using the power of God, and with Jesus, the miracle is done on *his own* power. Similarly, Elijah, even takes the boy's body into private, lies down on top of him, trying to get God to listen to his requests; in the Jesus story, Jesus simply touches the coffin: the magic is performed in public. The contrast between the two is that Jesus, as being fully God, performs this miracle with greater authority and with greater ease than Elijah. Luke's point is probably an argument to demonstrate to his audience that Jesus is greater than Elijah, but that the story remains in continuity with the prophetic tradition of the Jews.

Beyond these two points—that Jesus and Elijah's motivations are different, and that Jesus is more powerful than Elijah—is when the raising of the dead occurs in relation to when the boys died. For the Elijah story, the boy had just died. Conversely, in the Jesus story the boy's body had likely gone through all of the preparations for burial. Now, Jewish custom has four stages of its practices around the dead: first, the body is washed; second, there is a ritual purification of the body; third, there is the dressing of the body; and finally, there is the burial.

First, as soon as a person dies, Jews of this time would wrap the body in a sheet, which is then uncovered when the preparations are to begin. Second, the body is carefully washed, the hair slowly combed, the fingernails and toenails cut. Any wounds should be closed on the body and all jewelry is removed. Following the first washing, the body is then ritually immersed in water, or if this is not possible, water is ritually poured on the body as a means of purifying the body first of all dirt of this world and then ritually washing away the sin of the deceased. Then the body is dried and dressed in special burial clothing, usually with a sash with the Hebrew letter *shin,* which represents the word *Shaddai,* one of the names of God. The *shin* looks like a W, and also represents the word *shibboleth,* the word that the enemies of God could not pronounce in the book of Judges. Also: if you ever notice at the end of a worship service clergy sometimes give a hand gesture during the benediction that looks like Vulcan blessing sign from *Star Trek.* This is actually an ancient tradition, where the priest gives that blessing while making the letter *shin* with his hands.

After this, the coffin is prepared; if the deceased used a prayer shawl, the shawl is buried with the person, but the shawl is first torn on one corner to represent the fact that the body may no longer pray. Soil from Israel is then placed inside of the coffin, and once the coffin is sealed, it may not be reopened. Guards will sit and wait with the coffin until it is buried.

At the burial, men will take turns shoveling soil into the grave, three shovels at a time, as a means of giving a final gesture of goodwill to the deceased, and to end their grieving.

The burial customs of the time are pretty involved and have to follow a particular order, and are the traditions are very specific. If you know any Jews, you know how important proper burial is to their religion, and these customs can only be deviated with specific permission from a rabbi with authority.

\* \* \*

Here Jesus enters the scene. Remember that with Elijah, the burial practice hadn't begun yet, so no traditions have been broken. But with Jesus, we know that he has come to a funeral procession, where the body has already been washed, immersed, ritually cleansed, and prepared. The coffin is not to be opened under any conditions. The pallbearers stopped their procession, and the boy was brought back to life. Jesus interrupts what is not only a heartbreaking occasion, the burial of a child, but he is desecrating the burial practices of the boy in the process, and doing so with the authority of a rabbi who is above the laws of the religion.

When the Bible says next that everyone there "realized they were in a place of holy mystery, that God was at work among them," they acknowledged that this was no simple magic trick—the entire family had sat with the boy and combed his dead hair, trimmed his nails, and immersed him underwater. What just happened was an offense to their religion, but they also realized the great miracle in the new life of the son raised from the dead. The miracle of new life to this young boy came at the expense of tradition, custom, and the old religion.

This is as a metaphor for new life in Christ, "being born again." We have to die to our old selves, even carry out an elaborate funeral for our old ways if we need to—but Jesus does not just come to us as an expectation in ritual but Jesus *unexpectedly* comes to us and interrupts, *reverses* our lives. Often Jesus' entrance is unexpected and, in the case of the widow, Jesus might initially be seen as having come too late.

Beyond this, there is practical application to Jesus' *reversal* of tradition here. The people in the funeral procession were suddenly met with new life and made a decision to side with Jesus. They could have easily chosen to get mad at Jesus because they were in the middle of a burial custom that should never be interrupted, and the interruption of the burial could have a bad result on all of them in this life or the next. As it happens, Jesus' interruption *did* have, we can likely assume, a changed result for them for the rest of their lives, and for the next, because they witnessed the divinity of Jesus Christ on that day.

But this witnessing of the belief in Jesus did not simply lead people to follow the *status quo* or to keep doing business as usual. *Jesus radically interrupts and reverses the scene,* and in this case it is the community business of burying their dead. Those present looked at each other, and recognized that they were, as the Bible says, standing "in a place of holy mystery," and said among themselves, "God is back, looking out for the needs of his people!" This is the God of the people: placing people over profits, or people over land, people over elections, people over the rules. We may know that God as a God of the living and the dead, who cherishes human life as worth saving and worth living, and teaches us that the path to eternal life is one that begins in the death of the old self, and the baptism of the dead into new life in Christ. It is this necromancy that we live out as Christians every day.

## The Courage to Blaspheme
(Proper 10)
*Ephesians 6:12, Luke 10:25–37*

*This sermon was delivered shortly after the conclusion of the trial of George Zimmerman for the murder of Trayvon Martin; Zimmerman was found not guilty.*

My favorite line in the book and the film *The Last Temptation of Christ* reminds me of our Bible reading today, where Jesus is at the heart of his ministry, and he teaches everyone to "love your neighbor as yourself." Meanwhile, the Pharisees and lawyers in the distance yell at him, "that's blasphemy!"[1] Jesus looks up at those in the distance and proclaims, almost like a crazy man, "Don't you know who I am? I'm the king of blasphemy!" To the values and ethics of the world, the Gospel of love is the ultimate reversal of anything it can know.

In today's Bible reading, Jesus is bothered by a lawyer: who is ever happy when a lawyer comes asking questions? Now, how many of us are happy when a lawyer just appears to us out of nowhere and has some probing questions? But what makes a good lawyer is being able to ask good, loaded questions, so he asks Jesus what is perhaps an *unfair* question: "What do I have to do to get to Heaven?" That's one of the million-dollar questions, right? If we had one question to ask Jesus, I think many of us would ask just this. The trick question is that the lawyer asks Jesus an *absolute* question, and hopes to get Jesus' opinion, which would be open for debate.

Jesus responds with a question. If this were a courtroom, a judge would instruct Jesus to just answer the question, since the lawyer isn't on trial. Since this isn't a courtroom, Jesus asks the lawyer a pointed question in return: "you're a lawyer, and being a lawyer, you *surely* must know the law, so what do you say that the law says?"

The lawyer answers, "You shall love God with all your strength, and with all your mind, and your neighbors as yourself." The lawyer is directly quoting the Torah, Deuteronomy 6:5 and Leviticus 19:18.

Jesus then *affirms* the lawyer, and says, "Do this, and you will live." But since he has a lawyer there, and lawyers are known to not like the simple answers, Jesus answers with a parable, and goes on to say something quite *radical*.

Jesus then tells this parable, or story, of the Good Samaritan, which is a story we know well, but it is a story that we know so well that we hardly know it at all; we have watered it down to re-tell it to children so that *we have forgotten the blasphemy at its core.* Jesus' story goes like this. A man on the side of the road needs help and is "half dead." First, a priest walks by and ignores the man after seeing him. Of all people, the *priest,* who is someone who is not only an expert in the law, but a *practitioner* of the law, feels that he has no legal or religious obligation to help the man and keep going. Perhaps the priest here is avoiding the half-dead man out of a sense of ritual purity, and that the rabbi may even feel legally obligated to not help the half-dead man. Jesus here is clearly criticizing the religious leaders in the temple and their interpretation of the law, and is blaspheming against their religion.

Next, a Levite follows the priest and ignores the man on the road. The Levites are a tribe of Israel, who, according to Jewish history, were given cities of their own but were not given their own land when Joshua led the Israelites into Canaan. Even though the Levites did not formally have any land (they are believed to be direct descendants of Jacob, through his son, Levi), the Levites held a special place in Jewish tradition and law with special political responsibilities. Those who were part of tribes who were given land had to pay the Levites a tithe called the *masser rishon.* The Levites were primarily city-dwellers who were entitled to a welfare program funded by those who did farm the land. They of all people should be grateful to those roaming around the countryside, and certainly help one of those people who needs their help! But the snobby city dweller, like the priest before him, did not feel that the law requires him to stop and help the dying man!

To recap: The rabbi walks down the road and sees the half-dead man on the side of the road, and he says to himself: "I can't stop because the law says I shouldn't stop. It isn't like I am not stopping because I don't care, but because the law says that I should not." Then, the Levite comes by and says to himself: "The law doesn't require me to stop, and since every aspect of what I do and how I make my living is entrenched in the law, I am just going to do what the law says. If the law said I had to stop, I'd stop, but it doesn't say that, so I'm not going to stop."

Then the Good Samaritan arrived. The *good* Samaritan not only helped the man nominally, he treated him like someone whom he loved. The Samaritan nursed the half-dead man's wounds, and poured oil and wine on them—these were not commodities that you waste. Then the Samaritan put the half-dead man on his own animal, and walked with them and put him to a hotel. He pays to put him up at the inn. And he just didn't drop him off and pay the initial bill, the Bible tells us, the Samaritan took care of the man!

The Samaritan did this for a whole day, and then paid the hotel's front desk. He said that he would return later and pay for any other expenses that the man would incur.

*Who were the Samaritans?* What makes this story radical is that the Samaritans were considered by the mainstream Jews at the time to be ethnically Jewish, but the Samaritans practiced a different religion called Samaritanism. Since Samaritans were of a different religion, the *religious* Jews of the time believed the Samaritans to be heathens and outside of their own religion. Samaritanism was a religion that recognized the Jewish Torah, that is, the first books of the Old Testament, but interpreted it differently and did not recognize the authority of the Jewish priests. Samaritanism still exists as a religion today, and are still regarded as people of Jewish descent who practice a religion based upon the Torah. (Two pockets of them still exist in the city of Holon, which is just south of Tel Aviv, and around Mount Gerizim in the West Bank.)

That being said, the Jews during Jesus' time were suspicious of Samaritans, not only because the Samaritans were believed to have a false religion, but even worse, the Samaritans were believed to be Jews with a false religion based on Jewish scripture. Beyond this, King Herod the Great—the ruthless Roman client king of Judea who ordered the massacre of thousands of Jewish children in an act to get rid of Jesus as a baby—married a Samaritan woman named Malthace. Samaritans were believed to be traitors and were probably seen as being Jews who *sold out* to the political powers. Herod the Great and Malthace's son, Herod Antipas, was the tetrarch, or ruler of Galilee, during Jesus' time. This half-Samaritan Herod Antipas, we should recall, was one of the people whom the Bible tells us were responsible for condemning Jesus to death: he is the "Herod" of the Good Friday story who washes his hands of responsibility for Jesus' execution.

*It is no wonder* that the Samaritans were greatly disliked, which perhaps gives us a clue to why this story has been called the "Good Samaritan," perhaps implying that there must be at *least* one *Good* Samaritan!

Jesus concludes his story by letting the lawyer draw his own conclusions. "Which of these three, do you think was a neighbor to the half-dead man?" Jesus asked. The lawyer replied, "The one who showed him mercy." Then Jesus instructed, again affirming the lawyer, "Go and do likewise."

\* \* \*

The blasphemy of the story is astounding. First, Jesus says in his story plainly that those who are religious in nature, using the character of the priest, are so busy following the laws that they will not only carelessly ignore someone who is suffering but rather, those who pose as being religious prioritize their own religion over others' well-being. To go even further, Jesus implies that the legality of religion often defines the common good as something selfish, pretentious, safe, and self-serving. To be selfless, to do the *dangerous* or *risky* thing, to treat others like yourself might cause you to break religious laws. We can conclude from Jesus' parable that such a religion that even suggests that you do not treat others as yourself is a false religion.

Second, Jesus teaches that those who are outsiders are not only possibly very decent people, *but it's possible that a Samaritan may follow the heart of the scripture more than those with religious or social power*; that there is truth outside of the chosen few who are part of the mainstream, orthodox religion. Beyond this, it would seem that the *true* religion is *not* the mainstream religion, or even that human morality is higher than religious morality. Clearly, Jesus is blaspheming the heart of the practiced Judaism of his time.

We should be careful not to draw the conclusion that Jesus is *not* saying that his conclusion that religion must be blasphemed against is a blanket condemnation of Jews and Judaism as a whole. We should not conclude that this parable is making a blanket statement about one particular group. Instead, we should affirm that Jesus is making a statement about religion itself, that religion leads to false religion, and that all ideologies, all political ideas, all human experiences, all tribalisms have their own legalisms and fundamentalisms.

We are called today by our scripture to reject *false* religion, wherever and however expressed, and *blaspheme* against it, even and *especially* when it calls itself Christianity. If a religion, even indirectly, supports war, the limiting of human rights, promotes racism, or victimizes the poor, we must name it as evil and preach the Good News of Jesus, which for us today is the Good News of the story of the Good Samaritan. That is, we are to treat those who are knocked down, beaten up, exploited, shamed, and left for dead—those people who live all around us and are our neighbors—as ourselves, to treat them as unique, loved children of God who have *holy value* in God's eyes. If we are tempted to do otherwise, if we think we are too busy, too lazy, too frugal, or too selfish we must reject the culture and religion that teaches us this and treat others as ourselves, as Jesus instructs.

\*\*\*

In the late nineteenth century, the Danish philosopher Søren Kierkegaard wrote his final essays before his death, naming the corruption in the Danish government as evil, as well as how the Danish Lutheran Church simply endorsed the colonizing of other countries, looked the other way at political hypocrisy, and blessed the institutional corruption on every level of politics. Kierkegaard was one of the most Christian writers of his time, but explicitly repeated throughout his final writings that he would rather spit in the face of the so-called God of the Danish Lutheran Church than have anything to do with Christianity.[2]

In the past twelve hours we have heard the "not guilty" verdict in Florida for the George Zimmerman trial. As Christians grappling with the system of racial injustice, we are called to move beyond the recognition in this case of two young people of different races, who previously did not know each other, made terrible mistakes. And we are called today to move beyond leaving the justice and vengeance to just remain with God as passive participants in a system of divine justice.

Similarly, in this past week in the same state of Florida a black woman was sentenced to twenty years in prison for shooting a gun into a wall to scare away her abusive husband. No one died, no one was hurt. She claimed self-defense under the same Florida law ("Stand Your Ground") as George Zimmerman successfully claimed in his killing of Treyvon Martin.

It would appear that gun laws, as fuzzy and ambiguous as they are, don't apply to different kinds of people, apparently an abused black woman does not have the same protection of the law as others.

When we hear this parable of Jesus, we imagine the half-dead man along the side of the road as someone in a similar circumstance. But this parable does not just apply to half-dead men along sides of roads, but more broadly to those who are beat down by the system; those who feel the cold smack of injustice; those bleeding out to death on sidewalks, clinging onto candy wrappers; and those women and children whose abuse goes unnoticed by an ambivalent public.

We may, like the priest in Jesus' parable, say "I have no religious rule that compels me to work for justice." Like the Levite we might not care so much about the victims that we keep on walking because the one on the side of the road does not have the same ethnicity as me. We can just leave justice up to a court or to God to just sort it all out later.

But to be a Good Samaritan is to move past these temptations: to move beyond the lure of believing that our system of law is really blind to race and gender or the life that gun ownership is more important than the dead children who lie along the side of the road. We need to teach our children about God's justice by demonstrating with words and actions that we as a church are called by the Christ who bled to death on the cross to stand with bleeding victims, whose blood lines our streets *to work for a better world in the here and in the now.* A world where, as Jesus said, we love our neighbors as ourselves.

This is the same *heretical* or *blasphemous* foundation that we discover in Jesus' story of the Grand Samaritan: that we must often go *beyond* what our culture is telling us is the Christian way, or the Christian answer, or what it means to be a "Christian country." If it means abandoning what others tell us what it means to be Christian, in order to be a true Christian, to accept Jesus as a "personal lord and savior"; *if* we must abandon these things to *transcend* racial, social and economic boundaries to treat others as equals, then we must embrace the example of Jesus and find the courage to blaspheme.

## Boldly Prepared for 1950?
(Proper 15)
*Luke 12:49–56*

This teaching of Jesus is an especially challenging one, as Jesus proclaims that he is not bringing peace but bringing division: households will be divided, father against son, son against father, mother against daughter, mother-in-law against daughter-in-law, and so on. These words seem to contradict Jesus being the one who ends conflict, who ends wars.

Those who challenge Christianity today often cite the horror of our own history, the wars fought in the name of Christ, Christian nations who fought one another over petty squabbles, and the conflict of Islam that continues to this day. I recently finished my own personal study of the end of the Crusades and the early radical Protestant movements and what is shocking to me on some level is just how violent the conflicts between Protestants became at certain points in the earlier days of Protestantism. In fact, some Protestant groups started persecuting each other for the sole purpose of directing attention away from themselves so that the Catholics or some other group wouldn't persecute them anymore. This is to say, they *scapegoated* each other to keep themselves from being slaughtered.

So if Jesus was so great about bringing on peace, why hasn't it happened? This is the problem many see with Christianity: *you promise peace, yet your history shows violence.* Furthermore, many Christians today who talk about peace still talk about supporting war and continuing racism and homophobia, even in the same breath while they say they are against these things. All you have to do is read the letters pages to our local newspapers, or the Facebook pages of the local newspapers, to see what I am talking about. But this is the problem: Christianity promises peace, yet it seems by all accounts to have failed in ushering in peace. Perhaps the problem, then, is with the assumption that Christianity promises peace at all.

At the end of today's Jesus' teaching in the Gospel of Luke, he declares to all who would listen: "When you see a cloud rising in the west, you immediately say, 'It is going to rain'; and so it happens. And when you see the south wind blowing, you say, 'There will be scorching heat'; and it happens. You hypocrites! You know how to interpret the appearance of earth and sky, but why do you not know how to interpret the present time?"

The problem with expecting Christianity to bring about peace is that what we declare to be peace may be hardship or war with everyone else, and when we try to work for worldly benefits for ourselves, we typically do so by scapegoating others, by ignoring the evil we do to everyone else. This is true whenever we in the church look back to the 1950s as a time when the churches were strong, and new church buildings were constructed, and Sunday School wings were filled to the brim. This time of prosperity came about only through war and the results of the war, namely, that the median of wealth in this country was so far above and removed from the wealth of any other country that we could not see past our own good fortune to realize what we were doing to everyone else. And, we should remember that the era of *Leave it to Beaver* was only good for the middle and upper classes of white Americans.

We in the church lament the 1950s. We want to go back to it more fervently than anything else. Every time someone says "Since they got rid of prayer in schools," followed by some sort of problem, we create an idol out of the past to which we can never return, and we scapegoat everyone who has taken us away from the 1950s.

Since that era of history we have seen war after war. And internal conflict after internal conflict. And children killing children. And our own countrymen betraying our country. And, beyond this, we have a culture war around abortion, homosexuality, divorce, race, and sexual exploitation. There is conflict everywhere we go.

The church for many is a place where we leave these things at the door, or at least we pretend to leave these things at the door, for a safe haven away from it all. A safe haven that gives us the serenity of the 1950s, where Wally and the Beaver didn't have to worry about such things.

Jesus says that we say we can predict the weather, but we can't see the writing on the wall in our own present time. Jesus is not really ushering an era of peace, but bringing about an era of conflict, where we have to figure out how to move past the downward spiral of human selfishness and greed, and our lust for blood and death. *This is of enormous importance to understand the Gospel*: Jesus is instead giving us the tools to build the era of peace that is to come. The Kingdom of God is happening now, and will be brought into fruition in the future, but we cannot stand back as passive participants and complain about how it hasn't happened yet.

Jesus has instructed us of this elsewhere. There will be wars and rumors of wars. We will not always have Jesus with us, but the poor will remain with us. "Jesus" is not the answer to every question, but Jesus is the means by which we are to discover the answers to our problems.

The evidence is clear that thousands of years of history condemn the church's ability to bring about peace. The fact is that the times have been few when the world has lived up to Jesus' teachings of the beatitudes—blessed are the poor in spirit, blessed are those who mourn, blessed are the meek, and those who thirst for righteousness, and merciful, and pure of heart, and the peacemakers, and those who are persecuted (Matt. 5:3–10). We ourselves have been poisoned by our own limited conceptions of peace, success, and what it means to be "the church." We look backward into our recent past, a past before I was alive and a past many of you can relate to, and many are able look back with nostalgia. But do we want to be a church boldly prepared for the 1950s, or a church ready to engage the culture that we sometimes try to forget about when we enter these doors?

At the root of the problem, I believe, is the culture of "nice." When Jesus says that there will be division, he is not talking about pastors going on power trips, and he is not talking about churches forcing members to renounce family members to remain in good standing in the congregation—we all know people who have been in those situations. But Jesus is saying that fulfilling the mission of the gospel, to live out and practice the beatitudes in a way that does not resemble the Ten

Commandments or legalistic rules, is that sometimes a line in the sand has to be drawn. There must be uncomfortable times. There will be conflict. Jesus is not talking about picking up weapons, for the problems of the world can be solved through diplomacy and discussion—but nothing ever gets solved by being nice, and nothing ever gets solved by weapons. So the history of the world is that when we can't be nice, we grab our weapons. And when we put down our weapons, we try to be nice.

The Kingdom of God will come through conflict, the kind of conflict that makes people sweat on their upper lips and get uncomfortable in the seat. The kind of conflict that leads to calling out people when they do harm. The kind of conflict that takes our colleagues and peers aside and names the sexism and racism that goes on so often in broad daylight, to work for change. But just being nice doesn't solve anything. The language of Jesus in the Bible is very clear that he called those following him hypocrites in our reading this morning.

\* \* \*

In our daily routines we take Jesus' lure of getting offended for granted. We see too much exploitation of women, and too much commodification of young girls' bodies, and too much commercialization of childhood, and too much blaming of workers for working. We have a culture of blame and scapegoating of which it is so difficult to make sense that we have become immune to it. We are too busy with our first-world problems to deal with bigger issues.

Jesus calls his crowd hypocrites, and says that they can see all sorts of things happening around them but they can't see what is going on right in front of them. On CNN they used to have a special they would show on Sunday nights against the football games, which no one would watch, that would talk about what was going to happen in the news this week, giving previews of news stories *almost* ready to be published, mostly because the events in question fail the journalistic test of not actually happening yet. Yes, we can predict the news, we can predict the weather, next week's fashion, the buying trends for the coming months.

Our times are not so different from Jesus' times: we act like we can't even see what is happening right in front of us. We can see what is in front of us, but we distract ourselves from the present to concern ourselves with the future. And often we want that future to be something it cannot be, we want the future to be like the past.

I recently had a meeting with another pastor who is very upset, and kind of depressed at the state of the church at the end of his career. "When I was a kid," he said, "the church was everything. When I was a teenager, my life revolved around the church. . . . Now no one respects the church, no one respects pastors. They took prayer out of schools, and everything went bad."

I asked the pastor if he thinks that maybe his penchant for kicking people out of the church, and pushing for statements that clearly state that people are not welcome in the church might have something to do with the decline.

"No," he said, "Jesus called for division in the church."

I asked: "By telling everyone that if they don't believe exactly like I do, they can't be Christians?"

He lifted his head from talking to the floor in depression, smirked at me, and said, "If we just let anyone into the church we'd be like the United Church of Christ, now, wouldn't we?"

Some people just don't get it, don't they? *This* is exactly what I mean, and what I think Jesus is addressing, when he says that we can't assess our own present situation, that we want to boldly be prepared for the 1950s, as if Billy Graham is going to show up in town and make the 1950s happen again in 2013 or 2014. We're never comfortable with the here-and-now, and we always dismiss it, and by doing so, we dismiss those who need our help, and our prayers, and those who mourn and thirst for justice, and make peace *right now, and in the present moment.*

Regarding our current state of affairs, I ask: Is our faith in the risen Christ one that brings new life to those around us in the present, or is it looking to a future of reward in this life or the next? Does what we do now bring others joy in a way that expresses the love of God in radical and unexpected ways? Are we ready to reflect that love and practice the welcome that we put on our signs to the stranger? And are we ready to engage the culture that so many are looking for relief in the walls of the church and deeply make sense of it, and transform it from the inside-out?

## Why You Should Work on the Sabbath
(Proper 16)
*Isaiah 58:9b-14, Luke 13:10–17*

Jesus teaches in the synagogue on the Sabbath; while teaching, a hunched-over woman appears, and Jesus lays his hands on her and she immediately stands up straight and rejoices in God. The leaders, however, do not approve, accusing Jesus of breaking the commandment of Sabbath-keeping.

Jesus responds by naming them hypocrites, asking, do *you* not do *anything* on the Sabbath? And then you would deny this woman, who is one of your own people, a daughter of the same covenant, to be healed from the hold Satan has put upon her for eighteen years? Jesus' critics "were put to shame" and the crowd rejoiced. I kind of imagine that the audience's rejoicing began as a slow clap that then led to quite a bit of applause, and I suspect Jesus said what a lot of people were thinking.

Often when we think about the Sabbath, and observing the Sabbath, we consider it to be an abstention from work. It wasn't that long ago, when I was a teenager, that many of the malls were closed on Sundays, and many restaurants were closed on Sundays; in fact, some restaurants and chains today are closed on Sundays as part of their marketing scheme toward evangelical Christians and as an HR policy to their employees. One of my friends in high school worked for a grocery store that was closed on Sundays; the store offered their part-time employees who worked twenty hours per week bonus pay for taking off on Sundays—so that the part-time employees wouldn't feel the need to find extra employment on Sundays. This kind of business thinking is simply incomprehensible today; in fact, the movements to de-regulate alcohol sales and to allow hunting on Sundays in Pennsylvania today reflect what may be the last remnant of these "Blue Laws" in Pennsylvania.

As a child, one of the values that we had in our family was that Sunday was a day we did no yard work, and it was a day we kept the schedule pretty open to do things we wanted to do in the afternoons. My Sundays as a child and teenager were largely spent listening to the Phillies on the radio, reading, church activities, and playing in a community band. It never really occurred to me to go to the mall, so I remember as a teenager being quite surprised when I learned how to drive how little there is to do beyond resting on Sundays. In fact, the only kind of work we would do would be homework, but *only* if we couldn't finish it before Sunday. I had friends whose mothers would cook extra meals on Saturday so they wouldn't have to do much cooking on Sunday. Now, of course, in all cases it might be okay to go out to eat and have workers serve you, but you were not doing the working.

A woman once told me that when she was a little girl, she used to sew clothes for her dolls with a sewing machine. One Sunday, as she was making a dress for a doll, she sewed right through her fingers and had to go to the hospital for stitches. She told me that she'll always remember that after the whole ordeal was over, all her father could say was, "That's what you get for sewing on a Sunday."

All of this is to say so much of our thinking about "remembering the Sabbath and keeping it holy" and Sabbath-keeping is focused upon *not working* on the Sabbath. The history of the two-day weekend is actually a consequence of several factors—including the public school schedule and the labor movement—but the coincidence of Saturday and Sunday being known as our weekend came about because of the popularity of some Christians celebrating the Sabbath on Saturdays and not Sundays. (Some Christians still practice Sabbath on Saturday, most famously the Seventh-Day Adventists.) In parts of the U.S., as an act of tolerance, the weekend became a kind of Sabbath—*from work*—altogether to accommodate difference of opinion of which day is the proper Sabbath.

Today when we talk about the practice of keeping Sabbath, we often focus upon taking a pause from our overloaded and bloated schedules. Or taking a break from work entirely, which is difficult for many of us to do. Some people today talk about taking a Sabbath from social networking, or from technology, or even from politics—taking a break from those things that we know are consuming us whole but yet we typically just continue on with our addictions to them.

But this isn't what Jesus is addressing in his deconstruction of the Sabbath against the hypocrites in their own houses of worship. Jesus is saying that all of this thinking about the Sabbath, while not necessarily *bad* on face value, becomes *false* when we take it literally and legalistically. The synagogue leaders accuse him of breaking the covenants by healing someone who was sick; Jesus retorts that the covenant that is more important is that the hunched-over and sick woman is loved by God and is accepted by the love of God through her ancestral lineage to Abraham. So, then, which is more important: the legalistic thinking of the law, which many claim to follow in a serious way but few really do; or the law, the covenant, of God that seeks to open God's love to more than just a few people? Succinctly stated, is the law or covenants with God in history about *exclusion* or are they the practice of *inclusion?*

In answering we must first address that what we believe as Christians in this church is that God's sacrifice of Godself on the cross was an act that opens up the covenants made with Israel to everyone. An important act of God that is the Good News of Jesus is God's radical giving of Godself upon everyone, then further universalized on the Day of Pentecost with the Holy Spirit descending upon *all flesh*.[1] So the *work* of God in history is one of what is perceived to be an exclusive covenant moving toward something far more inclusive. It's worth mentioning that in the Gospel of John, for example, Jesus says that he is doing "God's work."[2] Work is not the issue here for Sabbath keeping, but more importantly, *the inclusive love of God is the work of God.*

This inclusive love of God is not new, but it has always been present from the beginning of creation. When we respond by proclaiming that the love of God is to be opened to those previously not allowed or barred from participation in the church, we are moving with the Spirit. The case is not that we, or we representing God, are "catching up" with culture; rather, *we as a culture are catching up with the movement of God in history.* God's love of the outsider is not anything new, but our response to that love may be new. Our changed minds about how liberal God is with love is not God's innovation, but our shift from our own inventions of conservatism and legalistic rules.

From the moment of creation, from the beginning of the very beginning, God's love is for all. We do not usually think this way about keeping Sabbath, but by virtue of the fact that we all rose from slumber and came to church for worship today is a ritual remembrance of creation. By worshiping on Sunday in community with others we are always remembering the collective memory of God's creation of the universe, since the Sabbath was God's crowning achievement: God rests on the Sabbath. We *respond* to God's resting on the Sabbath by, as the Commandments teach us, "keeping it holy." Keeping the Sabbath holy can involve rest, as we all know that we are in need of rest, and the Sabbath is the day we have put aside for worship. But keeping the Sabbath holy also means *doing the work of God*.

Jesus performs God's labor on the Sabbath, and the legalistic religious leaders condemn him for working. Jesus confronts them in their hypocrisy: Jesus does not claim that he's not working, for he is working. He's doing the *work of God* on the Sabbath. He is extending the mercy and love of God to someone who has been sick for eighteen years, who is regarded as having Satan in her by others—we should remember that those with chronic sickness like this were seen as unclean and were believed to have been afflicted by Satan as moral or religious punishment in their illness.[3] The one regarded as having Satan by the leaders is demonstrated to be a loved child of God by Jesus. The implication here is that the religious leaders, in their rules and policies and laws, themselves have Satan and practice Satanism by not recognizing the work of God, or disallowing the work of God on the Sabbath.

If our practice of Sabbath is a celebration of God the Father's work of creation, our *Sabbath work* is to continue this work of creation to be extending an inclusive message of God's love to the hardened hearts and filled ears of the past generations. What is missing from the religious leaders' legalistic understanding of Sabbath is precisely what we believe is being represented in Jesus' work on the Sabbath: healing a woman is deemed unclean and unworthy, a woman who had been socially shunned by the legalistic way of thinking about religion. When Jesus *radically reverses* the course of events, opening the door to the woman overcoming her social stigma, the gatekeepers attempt to close the door on Jesus.

But Jesus is known to open doors. Jesus opens the door for creation to be fulfilled and Jesus opens the doors of the hearts of the wicked and the sinful. Jesus invites the dead out of coffins and out of tombs. Our tradition teaches that Jesus opens the gates of Hell, and Jesus opens the tomb of death for himself, and opens that same door for us. Why is it so easy for Christians to close the doors of the Good News to others? I believe that it is our inability to see the Satan, the self-worshiping element of ourselves, working within us. As such, we as a people are called to open our own closed eyes, and walk through the doors Jesus has already opened for us. And in doing so, especially when it is reflected in our worship and religious practice in a way the influences our family, community, and business lives we continue the work of Christ. It is, so much as our traditions have denied and repressed such thinking, the labor that we should be performing on the Sabbath: our *Sabbath work*.[4]

## Huge Rummage Sale!
(Proper 18)
*Luke 14:25–33*

Jesus said, "None of you can become my disciple if you do not give up all of your possessions." We all have too many things. This passage of scripture from the Gospel of Luke is not just about giving up your possessions. Earlier, Jesus says that only those who hate their fathers and mothers, their brothers and sisters, and even hate life itself can follow him. Does Jesus really mean we have to hate our family and life itself? And then he says that we must pick up the cross and follow Jesus to be considered his disciples.

Remember that in Luke's narrative, this story takes place before the actual crucifixion of Jesus, and his statement, you must take up your own cross, has two meanings. The first is that Jesus is giving a hint to his audience as to what the future holds—and we should remember that all of the disciples also died horrible deaths. So there is something prophetic and quite literal about Jesus' words, which is to say, to follow Jesus is to follow him into his violent death and into the grave. The implication is that a resurrection awaits the other side of the grave.

But reading these words in context, we need to remember that the word "cross" or the idea of "crucifixion" were, for the Jews of the first century, absolutely unspeakable words. To say the word "cross" in public was abhorrent and was worse than swearing, it was giving language to the reality of the terrible persecution of the Jewish people at the hand of the Roman authorities. Just to utter the words *cross* or *crucifixion* would have caused people to faint or reject Jesus from the outset as a radical blasphemer because of his offensive language. What he was teaching, then, was not only politically radical, as in against Rome, and religiously heretical, that is, against the religious leaders, but *Jesus was assaulting the nature of language itself.* And we should remember that language was considered deeply sacred by the Jews; words were deeply important. The word "cross" was about the worst four-letter word you could say.

When Jesus says, then, to the multitudes of people following him, "you must pick up your cross and follow me," the audience had no idea what this meant in terms of Jesus' crucifixion, other than the likelihood that radicals and revolutionaries like him were destined to be executed on the cross. Furthermore, the audience heard him say words that before were *unspeakable*: if you want to follow me, you have to willing to offend every level of society from the top to the bottom, from the kings to your own mothers, fathers, sisters, and brothers.

It is within this context that Jesus' command to hate your mothers and fathers and siblings and life itself might make some sense. The institutions of paternity and family units—which are the building blocks of society and the Jewish understanding of the just society—according to Jesus must be undermined, reconsidered, and abolished. For Jesus, and through Jesus, *everything* in society must change. We all know what it is like when a couple gets married and the parents on both sides disapprove. The disapproving parents can choose whether to remain parents to children or to redefine what it means to be a parent; and if they choose the earlier there might not be children left to parent. Jesus is teaching us that following him requires us to leave people behind; it's easy to look at the king or the president or the senator and blame him for our problems and distance ourselves from them, but it is far more difficult and self-actualizing when we have to step away from someone close to us for our religious beliefs.

Now we all know that for some churches they mean this quite literally, and I know that some in this church have been involved in these kinds of exclusionary situations, where your choice to go to a certain church, or not go to a particular church, leads to conflict or even shunning. In fact, for some in my extended family, being a member or minister of the United Church of Christ has established me as an outsider. So common is this practice shunning within certain communities that they even call this one of their faith practices—some of us, for example, here in central Pennsylvania have surely met individuals who have been officially "shunned" from an Amish or Mennonite community. Jesus is not speaking about the practice of shunning, but rather he is talking about the radically new social order that he is envisioning and enacting. A New Order of *reversals*.

\* \* \*

Jesus directs you to hate life itself. This is a tough line to think through, and I actually thought about naming this sermon "Jesus was not pro-life" and posting it on the church sign. The question here is what Jesus means by "life" (when he says that you must hate life itself), and following our interpretation of this scripture about Jesus redefining relationships, Jesus is saying that clearly the *way of life* that we have become so *accustomed to* and *complacent within must change.* But going even beyond this, Jesus is saying, given the language of the cross, that there is a new kind of life, a new kind of existence, coming to us in the kingdom of God, that we will have to pass through the crucible of death to attain, that is far better than the one in which we are living.

That said, we should remember that Jesus is talking to people who were dirt poor, and it's quite likely that many of the people he was talking to were in the kind of cycle of poverty that we so often see in our country today, where family ties and family situations prohibit anyone from getting out of their current state of poverty. Being poor, politically oppressed, religiously repressed, and economically destitute, for Jesus to speak of a life that is better for them, where the rich are punished for their exploitation of the poor, and the poor are celebrated for their faithfulness to God, this kind of thinking clearly had some appeal.

Among the poorest of Jews, it was a common practice for them to live in a kind of clan-based communism, which is to say, everyone within their tribe and families shared the wealth. There were some wealthy and what me might call the middle class, but generally speaking by sharing their goods the extremes of poverty were somewhat minimized. (This practice of sharing goods is perhaps best illustrated by the prominence of the water well in these towns where Jesus traveled; most people shared their access to water, as only the wealthiest had their own wells.) The problem is that with centuries of war, persecution, and unfair taxation, the extremes of wealth became less extreme over time and there was less to share as the extremes of poverty became more commonplace.

By Jesus ordering everyone to give away their possessions, he is suggesting not only should people give more away, but that when you give away your possessions they should not be concerned with who is getting what. It doesn't matter if your possessions end up with someone from a different race or tribe. In other words, a new layer of communistic giving is being instituted where people who already shared everything were being instructed to give away everything. Jesus' command to give away your possessions is, on one level, a very practical commandment, which is to say, don't discriminate against people when you share your possessions.

\* \* \*

For the earliest Christian communities, a significant question arose when anyone with any wealth came into the church, so much so that they were reminded that Jesus' Gospel was a message for the poor and Good News for the poor. And what is Good News for the poor cannot also be Good News for the rich.

Tradition and scripture both seem to be speaking against most of us and most of our lifestyles, but also the church as a whole. Many of us know what the feeling is like to have a job, and then have it taken away, or to be in a relationship and to have that relationship taken away, or to have big plans and have those plans crushed. Most of the time, when these situations did not involve someone dying, we can look back at those times in our lives when God's communal grace was holding and surrounding us in our most exposed and vulnerable times. In cases where we have simply walked away from a career, or a lifestyle, or a home, or even a person whom we have loved, we either choose to be crushed by that loss or move on and try to find some liberation in the loss. Some of us are going through this right now, and we know it's not easy to talk about it while one is going through it.

But what Jesus is saying to us today, at least as a first step or a gentle step, is to assess the baggage that we are holding onto and get rid of it, and we will be surprised how much easier it is to be a Christian when we have less stuff holding us back. If we envision our lives going in one particular straight line, Jesus says, it's now time to make a sharp turn. And finally, we need to understand that for so many of us, growing up in the church and being part of the church our understanding of being a Christian is to live the straight and narrow path, the one that keeps polite company and maintains the status quo—and this was the Christianity I was also reared in—there could be nothing further away from the kind of religion of which Jesus plainly speaks in the Gospels.

So when is the big rummage sale?

## Lessons from the Grocery Store
(Proper 20)
*Luke 16:1–13*

Jesus tells a parable, a story of reversal: a small business owner gets word that his business manager has been cheating him of his profits. The owner immediately fires the manager, and afterward demands the books to be reviewed.

The manager, out of a job, then went from house to house of people who owed the owner money, and changed their bills so that they would be indebted to the manager.

When the owner found out about this, he praised the manager for his creativity in his scam. Jesus then explains that this is the kind of creativity, the creativity of desperate people out of work on the street, which he expects of his followers. To do whatever is really necessary to survive.

In our English translations, the business owner hears *"slander"* about the manager. The problem, however, is that the word "slander" in Greek is clear about the nature of the slander—in fact the word comes from the same word for "diabolical" or the devil. In other words, the rumor that the manager is stealing from the company is by its very definition, slander, which is to say, *not true*. The rumor was an evil rumor, a false rumor. The implication is that the manager was falsely accused and his boss just assumed his employees were cheating him and fired him without checking the facts: this is why Jesus clarifies that the owner fired the manager before checking the financial records later. Attention to this small detail changes the meaning of the story.

The falsely-accused manager goes out from his job, and *then* he cheats the owner, after being fired. The manager wasn't cheating his boss, at first, but then when the rumors began that he was cheating his boss, the manager assumes that if he's going to lose his job for stealing, he might as well get what he can out of the situation and cheat on his boss.

With his understanding of the story, it makes a little more sense that in the end the business owner gave some respect to the fired manager. It's kind of like when you watch gangster movies, that the godfathers respect each other because they recognize something of themselves in the other, even if they consider themselves enemies. In our Bible story the business owner might have recognized that he had it coming and that he had made a mistake in firing the manager in the first place.

* * *

When I was in high school, I began working as a cashier for the brand-new upscale grocery store. The store later changed hands and became a not-so-nice discount grocery store. The difference between the two different grocery store chains was immense; the nicer, first store was a much better company to work for, but the discount store prided itself on being employee-owned and being an employee-friendly company.

The reality was that with the satisfaction of the employees declining, the discount store quickly became a store in trouble. Many of their long-term employees left for similar jobs at other stores, including retail outlets in the same mini-mall. We regularly sat through mandatory trainings about employee theft. Lots of employees were fired for stealing from the store, so many that the store chain was bringing in other employees from other stores to keep the place going.

Through this I ended up getting trained to do just about every job in the store, because at one point they fired the whole deli department. I even became a customer service manager and then the night manager, and I continued to be the night manager every summer when I came home from college. And every summer I would train someone new to be the night manager, and that person would mysteriously disappear, and I would always have the night manager job back every summer when I came home from school. When I moved into management, I also caught employees stealing everything from food to cigarettes, and had to investigate some cashiers whose money was consistently off. As the store was about to fire nearly all of their cashiers they then found out that the person who had been counting the money in the office—and accusing everyone else of theft—was stealing right from the cashier's money tills! Needless to say, the store was a total mess.

Despite the problems, I liked working in the grocery store, and since I could do just about every job in the store, even when I was in seminary, if I came home from Chicago for a week I would come in and work a day or two just for some extra money. One summer I came home for about a month and put some time in as a cashier, and suddenly they needed a night manager again, so I did that. One night the cashier didn't show up for the night shift, so I ran the cash register while supervising the people loading the food on the shelves at night, it ended up that the cashier never came back again, so I did this for a week.

One of those nights a man came in and wrote a check. When we got checks we ran them through a machine, and the machine would approve the check, and we would be given a code to put on the check, and the check was then guaranteed. You've probably seen this machine or a similar process with writing checks somewhere. The man came in again that week and wrote a check, which was approved by the machine. I followed the same procedure, and the check was guaranteed to be good for the cigarettes. He came in a couple more times that week for cigarettes, and his check cleared every time. I just assumed that he was a regular. As far as I was concerned, so long as his checks were good, he could buy as many cigarettes as he wanted.

About a week later, on payday I was informed that someone from the corporate office of chain wanted to see me. I thought that this was great, I thought they were finally noticing the hard work I had put into the store, but then I suspected that something was up when I realized they were withholding my paycheck until the man from corporate came.

When I sat down with him, he opened his computer and showed me video of me checking this man out of the grocery line and asked me if I knew the man. I said I didn't know what I was talking about, and then he showed me video of the same man coming through my line a few days later. He said he was giving me one more chance to explain myself.

I assured him I didn't remember the man and I didn't know what he was talking about.

All of the man's checks bounced, and the corporate office thought I was working with the man to scam the store. I asked if they tried calling the man, his phone number was on the checks. He said no. I asked what the big deal was if the checks were insured because I ran them through the machine, and he said that they really don't bother with that. He came with a typed statement for me to sign admitting to guilt from stealing from the store. I refused to sign it, and he said that they would notify the police if I would not sign it, and when I said I wanted my paycheck and I wanted to leave, he refused to give my check and said that if I left they would call the police.

I reminded the man that I had worked well over 40 hours that week already so that I was happy to let him pay time and a half to me to let me sit in the office and look at him, because I was not going to sign a paper that I had stolen from the company. I asked him to call someone at the corporate office, because I didn't think it was fair to accuse me of this without even trying to get their money from this man. The fact was that it was easier for them to fire me than go after several bounced checks.

I sat in the office for about two hours and then the man from the corporate office came in again. He said, I've talked to your manager and he said you're in school to be a minister and that you've been working here for years and you've always been a good employee, and you've never been accused of any wrongdoing here. The only thing they had on my record beside good reviews was an injury report when I slipped and fell in the walk-in freezer when I was filling in as the frozen foods manager a couple years ago.

So he tore up the old paper he wanted me to sign and pulled another one out of his briefcase, and wrote my name in the blank space. The paper was a reprimand form stating that I admit that I did something wrong but that I would keep my job. I asked what I did wrong, and he said that I accepted two bad checks. I refused to sign that paper, as well, and he told me that I had no choice if I wanted to keep working for them. I told him

I would not sign any paper admitting guilt, and by this time I began to understand one of the reasons why the grocery store was so poorly run, namely, that the owners of the company assumed that their employees were constantly stealing from them.

The work environment there was so poisonous that the accusations led to people constantly stealing from the store. I know employees saw shoplifting and refused to report it because they said they were themselves afraid that they would be accused of stealing, I never understood this before, and now I did.

So I picked up my paycheck, wrote down my address to mail my final paycheck, and gave them the red smock that I had worn for years, and walked out. The store went out of business a few years later.

\* \* \*

*Jesus says that if you're honest with small things, you'll be honest with big things.* And if you're a crook in small things, you'll be a crook at big things. And so if the corporate office of a store creates a dishonest and distrustful work environment, the employees ultimately can't be trusted. And we know from our own practical experiences that this is true. Poisonous cultures create poisonous citizens and situations.

Jesus' story puts a sharp kind of judgment upon our culture and upon how we behave in the church. What is it about how we behave toward each other that creates a situation where we're not too surprised about absolute immorality within the church? How can we say we want to bring Christ to the world for salvation if we haven't really been sanctified ourselves, or the church? It's true that we inside of the church will always be a flawed because we are human, but this is something we need to figure out if we in this church are going to be truly effective in reaching the lost sheep in our community. And this is something for which we must seek the inspiration of God, and something for which we must seek healing of ourselves and within our community, nations, and families.

## You *Can* Take It with You!
(Proper 21)
*1 Timothy 6:6–19; Luke 16:14–31*

The conclusion of these passages of scripture is that money is the root of all evil. We know that the early Christians saw being wealthy as something that disqualified outsiders from entering the religion, and a good question would be, why would rich people want to be part of a religion that shunned wealth? And there is a trickiness to talking about wealth in the New Testament, because it is not the circumstance of being wealthy that is sinful but it is what one does with wealth, or how wealth makes people act is what is wrong with money.

This is a story that, for some reason, even given its obscurity in the Gospels, sticks in my memory from learning it in Sunday School as a teenager, because the imagery is kind of stunning and a little unusual. But if we take the story literally, it is one of the clearest visions of what the afterlife is going to be like. Jesus tells the story of Lazarus and the rich man. The rich man's "best friends" were the dogs, who would follow him around and lick his wounds. Lazarus would eat the scraps from the rich man's table. They both died and they can see each other in the afterlife: Lazarus in heaven being comforted by Abraham, and the rich man in Hell.

The image of Lazarus sitting with Abraham by his side is an image of a great feast; the implication is that the rich man feasted in this life, and now in the afterlife Lazarus is the one who feasts. He asks Lazarus to touch a wet finger on his tongue and comfort him in Hell, and Abraham intervenes, saying that a "chasm has been fixed" between heaven and Hell; reaching across is not possible. It's interesting that to say that it has been fixed, as the Bible does, suggesting that once a bridge was there. The rich man pleads that someone go back to tell his family of the torment that awaits them in the afterlife, and Abraham says that the scriptures say enough on the matter, and that even if someone came back from the dead, they would not heed his warning anyway.

Most scholars believe that while Jesus spoke in many parables, this story is not a parable because there is not an unexpected or hidden reversal in the story; rather the story is probably a folk take borrowed from another culture that Jesus changes a little bit so that his audience makes sense of it. One indication of this is Jesus use of the word "Hades" for Hell. Other first century writing by Christians and Jews uses the Greek word "Hades" in different ways, but the word Hades as a reference to Hell as a place of torment is specific to this story, having a lot in common with the ancient Greeks' religious use of the word.

The point is that this is probably a folk tale once told by the Greeks, and Jesus inserted Abraham into the story (perhaps in the place of Zeus). The story should not be understood in a literal way as saying something about the nature of Heaven and Hell, because this story isn't really about Heaven or Hell, it's about Hades, but more importantly, the story is really about money.

We might consider this story with jokes we have about heaven and Hell. You may have heard the one about the man who goes to heaven but doesn't like his accommodations. So he goes to St. Peter to ask to file a complaint. St. Peter said that there was a three year turnaround time for filing a complaint—and what's two years if you have an eternity, anyway?—so the man spends the next two years looking for a lawyer in heaven, and when he finally found one, he asked the lawyer to help him, and the lawyer in heaven suggests that he talk to the devil, since the devil is a kind of lawyer in the book of Job.

The man then goes to talk to the devil about his complaint. And the devil says that he would be happy to file a petition with God to have a change of venue for a trial, and that doing so would force God to change his accommodations.

The man was so happy and asked, "Where do I sign?" So the devil wrote up the papers and had the man sign his name in blood on the dotted line.

But he didn't read the fine print, which he realized as the devil was taking him to hell. "Why are you taking me to Hell?" he screamed.

"The only place we can change the venue for a hearing is in Hell," the devil said, "Because we have all of the judges!"[1]

Jesus' folk tale is a lot like this joke: the joke doesn't say anything about the real nature of Heaven or Hell, nor should the story be taken literally, but the message is very similar: money and power and corruption, and the drive to want more money, continue on into death.

It is often said that death is the great equalizer, the one thing that all people face, whether one is rich or poor, from one side of the world or the other. We all come into the world in the same way, we all leave the world, more or less, in a similar way. In Jesus' story, death is *not* an equalizing force; instead, the afterlife should be understood as revealing the bare reality which is latently and obviously present right now. In other words, a tremendous gulf continues between the rich man and Lazarus in the afterlife, just as there was in this life. Lazarus was followed around by dogs in this life, but those who lived righteously will congregation with righteous in the next life, those who are wicked will in the next life be cloistered with the wicked.

Lazarus probably asked the rich to help him with food or small amounts of money, and the rich man could not for a variety of reasons. There was surely a big wall between the rich man and the poor man, not only the wall between where the rich man slept in a nice bed and the streets upon which Lazarus laid his head, but a big wall of excuses of why he couldn't help the poor man. The rich man knew of richer people, and probably defined himself as middle class, so being middle class, he likely felt that he doesn't have as much responsibility as someone else to help those with less.

We all dig moats between ourselves and those we perceive to be poorer than us, as well as building up a wall of resentment toward those who we perceive as being wealthier than us. Jesus' folk tale about Lazarus and the rich man suggests to us that these walls that we build up now, lead to chasms between us and being reunited or comforted by God later, and furthermore, even if someone came back from the dead—perhaps even Jesus himself—to show us otherwise, we still wouldn't listen. Those walls are just too big and too great that we blind the social realities of the world to us by hiding the truth from ourselves, so all we can see around us is the walls on either side of us.

\* \* \*

We have all heard it said about money that "You can't take it with you." What Jesus' story is saying is that *there are ways to take money with you into the grave,* because the effects of money, that is, building walls to shield and hide the reality of the world, the spiritual consequences of how we use and abuse our wealth, continue with us. What we do with the money, and how money dictates our actions matters far more than the quantity of money that we have.

Finally, have you ever considered that the way we talk and act around money reflects a religion around money? It's not polite to talk about money or religion at dinner parties. There is a whole language about how money works that investors and economists use which is similar to the technical language that theologians use to talk about religion. Money is "backed" by gold, or at least it used to be, and now we just need to have faith in the value of whatever systems "back up" the money, just as many people believe their faith is rooted in a God or in a scripture, whose origins and presence now seems to have dissipated or is up for debate. We can talk about having happiness in the acquisition of money or with religion. And the way our global markets and behaviors are dictated by the imaginary swaying and shifting of financial interests reflects how we often think the world should act around God.

In fact, the consumer confidence index that so often gets talked about is really measuring our faith in the economy, our faith in money, our faith in being able to get some money, or the faith that we will in the future have more money to pay for things we may or may not need. How we make choices about spending money is about the faith, sometimes the false faith, we have in whether we can pay the bill. If we make good choices about money, money can sometimes reward us with credit, and if we make bad choices with money, many people are rewarded with an abundance of credit they should never deserve. They are then in an eternal debt that never seems to get paid off—so often the language of Christianity is about our paying off debts, specifically the debt for sin that we can never totally be paid, no matter how much religious credit we have. The end game of the religion of money sounds similar to the way we think about heaven: moving into a big mansion and having everything we want. We can probably determine person's a values by looking at the memo of his or her checkbook.

Yet at the same time, so much of the core of the Jesus' message is quite plain that part of the empire that needs to topple for the reign of God to occur is wrapped up in matters of money, and money is the control mechanism of the political powers to dictate the behavior of the masses. We all know that Marx said that religion is the opium of the people, but if we look around to how the world really works, money is the opium of the people, so often when it behaves very much like a religion.

This, I believe, is what Jesus meant when he used the language of "debts" and the forgiveness of our "debtors" in the Lord's Prayer, right after the petition that we be given "our daily bread" by God alone. This prayer that we say so often, that we hardly know it, speaks plainly the reversal which Jesus' story suggests: that money has everything to do with our faith, and the choices we make with our money that may seem wise in the here and now, are foolish in the eyes of God and in the building of the kingdom of God.

We conclude the Lord's Prayer with the words "For thine is the kingdom, and the power, and the glory, forever." The lines leading up to it about daily bread, forgiving debts and debtors, and being delivered from evil, and the power of God are all connected on this issue. We pray not to the emperor, as was expected of the Jews by the government who issued currency, and we do not make a God out of our government, but rather, God, who does not issue currency, receives the power and glory by those who pray to him, who look to him for dependence rather than placing their faith into systems of money.[2]

## Judas Priest!
(Reign of Christ / Christ the King Sunday)
Jeremiah 23:1–6, Luke 23:33–43

Today is Christ the King Sunday, which is the final Sunday of the church year. You probably know that our secular calendar, the one that runs from January through December, is a pagan calendar from the Roman Empire. But in the Christian calendar this Sunday is the final Sunday of the year, next Sunday is like New Year's Day, as the first Sunday of Advent, a time of preparation for Christmas.

The Bible reading for Christ the King Sunday is this well-known scene from the death of Jesus, which one would think is a more appropriate Bible reading for Good Friday. But here we find Jesus, hanging on the cross, being mocked by his fellow Jews, and being executed by the Roman Empire.

Imagine: Jesus' arms are outstretched on the cross. Our art usually shows Jesus being partially clothed, but that was unlikely, he was probably naked when he was crucified. Crucifixion was a kind of death only reserved for the worst criminals and it was a kind of torture meant to be an insult. So much of the Gospel of Luke is about how outsiders of society of the temple are really God's insiders—if you've been listening to me preach for the last year, this is one of the primary messages of Luke's Gospel—but here Jesus is outcast by his own race, his own religion, and we should remember that the Temple priests were really puppets of the Roman government. Everyone is involved here, but Jesus is the victim of a state execution.

Jesus is outcast by the angry mob, and we know how often angry mobs can be dangerous, both physically and politically; but most importantly Jesus dies as an outcast from his ruling Empire, the government rules that he is too dangerous to be kept alive and he is executed. Jesus spent one night on death row and was ordered to be executed. We should never forget that the crucifixion is an act of capital punishment and it is the act of a government too large and too far removed from the real people living on the ground that it does not really care who is executed and why. Jesus belongs to a rowdy religious and oppressed minority, and the Roman government is trying to keep the peace, because it seems that everyone else wanted Jesus dead.

But then we have Jesus blessing a criminal on the cross. We don't really know what these criminals did but they probably did *something* wrong to end up on the cross, and even they recognize this while hanging with their arms and feet nailed to the cross, nude, and waiting for the birds to come and start pecking at their eyes and the dogs to come to eat at their feet.

The way Luke tells the story, one criminal, having a cold heart, mocks Jesus with the rest of the crowd—you would wonder why he would do that, but I imagine this man as kind of like a bully, that the only dignity that he sees himself having left is to belittle Jesus while he himself is dying, so as to take away his own crime and the spectacle of his own punishment. It is interesting to me that this criminal is placing his sins from his own crucifixion onto the other, which is in essence what we believe we do with our own sins—we hand them over to the atonement of Jesus on the cross, God's death.

But then the other criminal says that Jesus doesn't deserve this, and suddenly recognizes that Jesus is the messiah, and asks his famous line, "Jesus, remember me when you enter into your kingdom." Jesus responds, "today you will join me in paradise."

Traditional Christianity holds that Jesus did not go to heaven at his death, but he went to hell, and there confronted the devil and opened the gates of hell before returning on Easter to show that he had not only come back from the dead, but had descended and returned from the darkest depths of humanity, in Hell—we often don't talk about this much but it's even in some of our favorite Easter Songs, such as in "He arose": He "came from the dark domain," the song sings. Is Jesus saying that the man on the cross will join him in Hell or in Heaven? The Bible says that he will join him in paradise.

Only through knowing the depths of our own sinfulness and our dire human condition can we truly know what a resurrection is, let alone know of Christ's resurrection. Some of us know this well, that it is when we felt the lowest points in our lives when we feel God the closest, or we can at least look back at God's hand upon us during a time when we might have even experienced God as absent—we were just caught up in everything else going on that we couldn't notice God working with us and through us. *The courage to be is usually known only in hindsight.*

\* \* \*

As I have pondered over this passage of scripture I kept focusing my thoughts on the fact that the first one to enter into Christ's kingdom, whatever it might mean, is a criminal. He probably killed someone or stole from someone important. He might not have deserved the death penalty in our eyes, but Jesus was executed anyway. Jesus broke the law of both the Empire and the Temple. In the eyes of the law, he was a criminal.

And while thinking about this last week, I kept thinking of this guy who ended up living next door to me for two years in college, his name was Fred. Fred was so nervous and neurotic he lost all of his hair at age 18 and he constantly chewed off his fingernails. About once every two or three weeks he would just have a meltdown in his dorm room, often prompted by something simple, like the cafeteria being out of the particular cereal that he liked to eat, and he would skip his classes and lock himself in his room for hours. Eventually I would hear the Judas Priest song, "Breaking the Law," loudly coming out of his room. The song kept repeating its title—"Breaking the Law"—over and over again as its chorus.

The first time I heard this, I heard him in his room just yelling at himself for several hours, and then the music started. The song would repeat, over and over again, and I could hear Fred yelling the words "Breakin' the law, breakin' the law" over and over. And then I would hear banging sounds. At first it sounded like books being thrown, and then it sounded like his clothing dresser, and then it sounded like things shattering. So I went out of my dorm room, and there in the hallway a group of people had gathered, listening to him trash his dorm room with the Judas Priest song blaring on eleven.

We decided to knock on the door, which we had to do several times so Fred would hear us knocking. Eventually the music went off, and then he cracked open the door, and he peeked out his head and said, as if nothing was going on, "Hey guys, what's up?"

We all said, "Fred, are you all right?"

He just looked down and said, "Yeah, I'm all right. Everything is just all right." And then he shut the door quietly and locked it.

Everyone out in the hallway just looked at each other and shrugged our shoulders, and as we were about to walk away, we heard the music come on again, "Breakin' the law, breakin' the law!" And Fred was yelling with it. Shortly thereafter I again started to hear things being thrown: I am pretty sure I heard the television smash on the floor and the bunk beds falling onto the floor.

Later that evening, my friends and I ran into Fred, and we asked if he was okay. He said, yeah, why do you ask? And then he went on as normal, in fact, he was happy as ever.

Later I asked one of his former roommates about this, Fred would get roommates and they would always leave the dorm or quit school, and he said that Fred would do this every couple weeks and then he'd be fine, but then he would have a breakdown and have to trash the room again. In fact, his roommate said that Fred would often trash the room and then go to Catholic mass all day on Sunday, and it was almost like trashing the dorm room and singing "Breaking the Law" was a pre-Eucharistic preparation for church on Sunday.

Later I had a class with Fred, and we had to work on a project together, and I asked him about trashing his room. He didn't really say much about it, but I also learned that behind this quirk, Fred was very, very religious, and he volunteered quite a bit in various soup kitchens—in fact, he spent more time volunteering than any other college student I knew. He told me once that when he gets angry at the world, he simply goes to mass, and everything is all right. But he ended up going to mass nearly every single day during many weeks. Fred was an outcast, but the one place he found acceptance was church.

Clearly, regularly trashing a dorm room is not normal behavior, but I like this story as it offers a good image for the image of the kingdom, the kingdom where Jesus is king, Jesus as Lord of the Outsiders. Jesus is the king of all who have hit rock-bottom, and Jesus is king of all of those who suffer. He is the king of the widow and the widower, the king of the fatherless and the motherless, and he is king of the poor and the rich who sacrifice for the sake of the children of God. He is Fred's king.

Consequently, Jesus is *not* the king of those who mock and bully the oppressed. Jesus is *not* the king of the religious zealot who wishes to enforce his beliefs upon everyone else. Jesus is *not* the king of the dishonest politician. Jesus is *not* the king of the rich whose wealth has convinced them that they have been blessed by God for their own good deeds and are in no need no salvation. The scriptures teach us over and over again that Jesus prefers the company of the poor and the outsider, the repressed and the oppressed. And finally Jesus invites a criminal dying with him the worst possible death humanly possible to enter into his kingdom.

The Jesus who is coming back to make the world right is the Christ whose followers have hit rock bottom at some point and know that it is through the bottomlessness of desperation that Christ returns to us. We have to know what it is like to be a criminal, to be the sinner, to break the law, to be able to bounce back and appreciate the journey we have been on, and *it is the risen Christ who meets us when we return, because he is a God of resurrection and regeneration.* Jesus transfigures us and holds us close to him when we are at a total loss.

This is where we leave this past church year, as today is the last Sunday of the Christian year. But in this contrast between utter despair on the cross and the triumph of Christ as the King of heaven, we enter into this coming week with Thanksgiving, a time to appreciate the things that really matter to us, and then the season of Advent, which is a new year, but Advent is also a time of preparation for Jesus to come to us as a baby in a manger. So this end of the year is a new opportunity to begin anew and to give ourselves to God one more time, understanding that committing ourselves to Christ is not a one-time event, but one which we must do continuously and in new ways throughout our lives. As we cross this liminal space into Advent, we seek the king who arrives to us in dead midwinter as a child in a manger, homeless, born to unwed single parents, who were themselves running from the law and running for their lives. Jesus is born a criminal—and he dies a criminal.

So before his death, Jesus says to the criminal that he will be the first to enter into paradise with him. Knowing that first Jesus will pass through the crucible of Hell, Jesus invites a hardened but repentant criminal to accompany him: if you're going to Hell to open the gates, you don't necessarily want a goodie-two-shoes as your sidekick. The Good News for us is that Jesus saves sinners, and extends the invitation to the criminal—those who break the law—and saves us, speaking to us as criminals who know the depths and the lowest points of human experience.

## How Christian is Thanksgiving?
(Thanksgiving Day)
*Matthew 6:5–15*

*This sermon was initially preached by invitation at an ecumenical Thanksgiving service, held at a Roman Catholic Church in Central Pennsylvania.*

I have a confession to make: I am a little ambivalent about Thanksgiving: I love Thanksgiving, but I am a bit torn about its history. Thanksgiving is one of the few holidays that has become completely commercialized, and it's one of the few holidays that just about all Americans can agree on. In fact, just about everybody eats the same thing on Thanksgiving, even people who don't particularly care for turkey eat it. In fact, the only time I have ever seen my father eat poultry has been on Thanksgiving, it's kind of like sauerkraut on New Year's Day, that if you don't eat it it's not just bad luck, but when it comes to Thanksgiving and turkey, it's anti-American and communist to not eat turkey.

Even though I was baptized in the Evangelical Congregational Church, and was confirmed as a United Methodist, and went to a Catholic college, and went to a traditionally Baptist seminary, and then did doctoral work at a Unitarian theological school, I was ordained in the United Church of Christ, and I can appreciate that Thanksgiving is a very UCC holiday. The pilgrims who sat down for a meal with the Native Americans are my adopted denominational forebears, and it seems that this very UCC tradition has been extended to everyone. But history is not so simple.

The first thanksgiving was actually held in the Colony of Virginia, to be celebrated on December 4 to mark the day of the arrival of the English settlers in the area north of Jamestown in 1619. Thanksgiving was certainly bad news for the Native Americans and the holiday was meant to celebrate English manifest destiny over the new world. This was two years before the Thanksgiving celebrated in New England that we all know about so much better.

The thanksgiving involving the Congregationalists and the Native Americans happened in 1621, again, two years later, at Plymouth Plantation. There is some debate as to the details of the first Thanksgiving Day, but the day was a religious observance of thanksgiving, of *survival,* because had the Native Americans not given them food and had they not taught them how to harvest corn and catch eel, the Pilgrim settlers would have likely died off. The Massachusetts Bay Colony began celebrating thanksgiving irregularly, beginning in 1630, and then in 1680 Thanksgiving became an annual holiday.

Other colonies celebrated Thanksgiving holidays, but they were days of remembrance of local military victories. Those days were not feast days but days of fasting, in fact in December, 1777, the first national day of thanksgiving was held by all of the colonies to remember the British surrender at Saratoga. The Continental Congress designated December 18 to be a celebration of the end of the Revolutionary War. The tradition continued from there that the President had to declare a thanksgiving every year. President John Adams proclaimed two Thanksgivings during his presidency, but Thomas Jefferson did not declare any. In 1814, President James Madison revived the tradition of Thanksgiving as a response to the conclusion of the War of 1812. Madison would declare two more Thanksgivings, but none would be held in the autumn, and in 1816 some states in the north had Thanksgivings in their states only, but they were held on different days. The following year, in 1817, the state of New York became the first to declare it a regularly scheduled state holiday.

The southern states refused to practice Thanksgivings and many Southerners resented the practice of celebrating Thanksgiving, as the myth of the Pilgrims eating with the Indians became more prevalent in American culture. The Southerners actually saw the practice of remembering the Pilgrims to be too pro-Northerner, too hypocritical. I also suspect that there was a deep racism underneath their dislike of the holiday, so as to imagine the re-enactment of sitting down to share a meal with Indians was unthinkable, and they, again, saw the northerners' practice of Thanksgiving to be a bit dishonest.

As a further insult to the South, and as an act of unity, President Lincoln declared that Thanksgiving should be practiced on the final Thursday of November every year, beginning in 1863. This tradition held until 1939 when President Roosevelt was pressured by the owner of the Federated Department Store Corporation, now known as Macy's, to push Thanksgiving earlier for when the final Thursday of November was a fifth Thursday, meaning that there would be less shopping days between Thanksgiving and Christmas (just like this year). The Republican Party cried foul, not because of the corporate interests but because they said that Roosevelt wanting to change a law Lincoln had set was "Anti-Lincoln," and people of different political persuasions went against the President Roosevelt's order to change the date, so that there was a "Democrat Thanksgiving" and a "Republican Thanksgiving." The Democrat Thanksgiving became known after the president's name, "Franksgiving."

This was so controversial that in 1941, both houses of Congress had a special session just to fix the Thanksgiving problem, and now it is federal law that Thanksgiving always be the fourth Thursday of November.

So while Thanksgiving may not have been culturally ruined in our culture, it is true that the politicians have ruined it, but these events are so long ago that we have forgotten about them.

\* \* \*

As I just mentioned, in 1863, Lincoln made the final Thursday of November to be Thanksgiving, and in 1864, the following year, Thanksgiving fell on Thursday, November 24. In the days coming to Thanksgiving, U.S. Army Colonel John Chivington, a Methodist preacher, used his political and religious connections to convince the governor of Colorado, John Evans, to give the native Americans, who were in constant conflict with the locals, to have a special piece of land as a gesture of peace, after Black Kettle, the Indian chief of the Northern

Cheyenne attempted to work a peace agreement. The Native Americans were instructed that they would always be safe in this area, called Sand Creek, if they rose the American Flag over their lodge.

On the night of November 28, 1846, three days after Thanksgiving, the Indians were attacked by a militia headed by the preacher John Chivington, and with the approval of the governor John Evans, after a night of heavy drinking. What ensued was one of the bloodiest events in American history. Nearly all of the Indian nation were killed, but not just killed. They were mutilated and dismembered, including the women and children. Within a few hours, as many as 500–600 Indians were killed. Only three survived the attack.

And then, the men took their bodies and impaled the bodies and parts of their bodies on spears, sticks, and bayonets, and paraded them through the streets of downtown Denver. Everything from heads, hands, male and female genitalia, and even fetuses taken from the bodies of the women, were paraded and then put on display in the Apollo Theater and some downtown saloons in Denver. *This was the first Thanksgiving Parade.*

A panel convened in our federal government to investigate the whole incident. One of the military men who offered testimony against the mob who did this horrendous event was killed when he returned back to Denver. The remainder of the survivors were declared to receive reparations for this act of genocide, but no payments were ever made. What made this atrocious act even more offensive is that forty-five years later, in 1909, a Civil War monument was installed on the grounds of the Colorado State Capitol, and the monument lists the battles of the Civil War fought by Colorado military units, and it included Sand Creek, 1864, as one of those battles, which, of course, we know had nothing to do with the Civil War.

My ambivalence about Thanksgiving has more to do with the fact that we remember sitting down to eat with Indians, *only to massacre them later.* One eyewitness of the parade of dismembered bodies in Denver wrote the following:

Jus to think of that dog Chivington and his dirty hounds, up thar at Sand Creek. His men shot down squaws, and blew the brains out of innocent children. You call such soldiers Christians, do ye? And the Indians savages? What der yer 'spose our Heavenly Father, who made both them and us, thinks of these things?

It is true that in the second year that Thanksgiving, as we know it, was a federal holiday, in the year after it was made law by President Lincoln, in 1864, Christian men conspired to give the Native Americans a safe place, and set them up to be massacred, dismembered, and mutilated, and their remains put on display. If we are dishonest about this day, we continue the atrocities committed by our Christian forebears.

\* \* \*

When we pray the Jesus prayer, the "Our Father," we must recognize it as *a prayer of reversals,* beginning by blaspheming the name of God by calling God "daddy" as an insult to the Temple leadership of his time, and ending with an offense to the Empire which occupied his people, saying, "for thine is the kingdom, and the power, and the glory forever." When we pray this prayer, we often say it was words of comfort or repetition, and we don't think about just how radical these words are.

So when we pray the prayer of Jesus, the "Our Father" prayer, we pray that God forgive us our debts, as we forgive our debtors. The Good News that I have to preach today, if we are to take the prayer of Jesus seriously and our own traditions of Thanksgiving honestly, is that Thanksgiving is an invitation to enact the Kingdom of God in the here and now by rendering it an act of reconciliation. That this day be an act of truth telling, of honesty, of authenticity, and ultimately be an act of forgiveness seeking forgiveness. That Thanksgiving be a day of settling differences, and teaching our children about our past mistakes—whether it is in our families or as a nation—and that our expectation is that we have the grace to move toward a new perfection and that we raise our children to transcend our past and current mistakes of racism, of classism, and of discrimination and genocide of all stripes.

We need to proclaim boldly in Christian churches—and if I may use this opportunity as the first time I've ever spoken from a Catholic pulpit—that God expects better of us, and that this is our opportunity to say it loud and teach it to our children, that our God is a God who, as we celebrate during Advent, takes on the depth of our flesh, and embodies all of us and our mistakes. As an act of reconciliation, Thanksgiving is our opportunity to work toward God finding us worthy of forgiveness, and doing the work, especially when the work is hard, of creating a world that is truly a Kingdom of God for those who have been on the receiving end of injustice. *The reconciliation is part of the incarnation.* This is an invitation to realize that we have *not* yet arrived in a state of being worthy of forgiveness for our nation's sins, and that our plentifulness, our wealth, our privilege, our deaf ears to reason and the cries of poverty, and our mute mouths to speak for those whose tongues are only filled with sorrow.

Thanksgiving is the day for us to realize that every day we do not do these things, we blaspheme the God known to us as "Our Father" in the Jesus prayer, we, in essence, deny the resurrection of Christ by denying our bodies and actions to be bearers of the cross and the sites of the resurrection in the present.

Let us enter into this Thanksgiving day, which is a happy day of pause, and a happy day of family and food, as well as a somber day remembering those who once shared our table but who are no longer present to us; *it is a day re-membering the dis-memberment of Christ, and also re-membering the dis-memberment of those our culture has abused and forgotten.* Let us re-member that we, as the body of Christ, are broken, as we re-member that which we do in re-membrance of the one who leads us to re-member and act for justice in the world. So that we may affirm the Good News of Jesus, and proclaim it from the mountaintop, and teach it to our children so they do not forget, that this is a time for us to be the Body of Christ, and to work for a greater union of all of humanity, in a world and in our country that is so bitterly divided and broken.

# Afterword

What would it mean to preach the "death of God"? Or why would one even entertain the prospect? On the surface the title of Chris Rodkey's beautiful and brilliantly crafted set of sermons, which were actually delivered to mainline Christian congregations, would seem to be simply a parody of the prerogatives of ministry, a fashionable play on what for the past several decades has been an equally fashionable set of themes in academic theology. Ever since Thomas J. J. Altizer, a youthful and incendiary professor at Emory University, proclaimed in the mid-1960s that Nietzsche's infamous dictum that "God is dead" actually encapsulated the covert meaning of the Gospels themselves, the theme has been served as a permanent provocation and conceptual allure for Christian thinkers and professional practitioners disenchanted with the substantiality and sustainability of the present day Jesus industry.

But what if "preaching the death of God" were not simply a chic twist on standard, everyday progressive messaging to the ecclesiastical faithful, but the very heart of the Gospel itself? For Altizer, the wry trope of "God's death" has always signified what is really at stake when we say, in contradiction to Gnostics, Muslims, and assorted Christian Docetists, that God "died" on the Cross. The brutality of crucifixion as practiced by the Romans was deliberately designed as a penal method that sought to confirm a total annihilation of the victim's dignity and personhood as well elemental humanity. It was predicated on the assumption that *Romanitas* equals *humanitas,* that anyone who challenges this equation—and the vast majority of victims of crucifixion were accused of various crimes against the state—must be consigned to zone of absolute nothingness.

For God to "die" in this way means that the divine itself has passed fatefully over what the religious mind would consider the threshold of everything that is *not-God*. Nietzsche was not the first to articulate this insight. Fragmentary sentiments to this effect can be found in the writings of the late Medieval mystics, in the sayings of Luther and his embrace of a *theologia crucis,* and of course in the great philosopher G.W.F. Hegel himself who took up this theme in the last chapters of his *Phenomenology of Spirit.* These thinkers were not restless renegades, the "bad boys" of a durable tradition, which has been tolerant of such conceptual innovations, but hardly acquiescent. They knew their Scripture. Each in their own way had aimed to rescue Christianity from its long "captivity" in the Babylon of Greek metaphysics. They knew that it was not a simply choice between Athens and Jerusalem, but between the Jerusalem with its sacred confinement of an infinite God within the Temple site and the abjection of God himself as a tortured body on display at the entrance to the city, as an outlaw and outcast, as an evanescent presence that has been totally "profaned" (from the Latin *pro-fanum,* "outside the temple").

The one who "preached" the God's "death" in this sense, of course, the apostle Paul. Throughout history the business of theology—whether it be confessional, exegetical, or constructive— has been to explicate the intimate interconnections between *theos* and *logos,* to start with a certain *factum* of religious life, experience, or collective memory and develop its deeper significance as well as its broader implications. The theological enterprise has always inscribed itself within the order of cultivated general knowledge, with *sophia* as the kind of discerning and critical intelligence that is able to arrive at universal truths. Thus the "death of God," let alone a "death of God theology," violates the very premises of what is normally considered theological thought overall. Thus when Paul proclaims in the first chapter of 1 Corinthians that it is his calling to preach "Christ crucified," he is saying something that calls into question the usefulness of the familiar dichotomy between Jerusalem and Athens:

For the word of the cross is foolishness to those who are perishing, but to us who are being saved it is the power of God. For it is written,

'I WILL DESTROY THE WISDOM OF THE WISE,
AND THE CLEVERNESS OF THE CLEVER I WILL SET ASIDE.'

Where is the wise man? Where is the scribe? Where is the debater of this age? Has not God made foolish the wisdom of the world? For since in the wisdom of God the world through its wisdom did not *come to* know God, God was well-pleased through the foolishness of the message preached to save those who believe. For indeed Jews ask for signs and Greeks search for wisdom; but we preach Christ crucified, to Jews a stumbling block and to Gentiles foolishness.[1]

One could read this passage, as many pious and simple Christians have done for centuries, as a rejection of advanced learning as having any real value in living out of one's faith. For does not Paul's witness condemn the "wise ones" (*tes sophias*) and commend those who are "foolish" (*tes morias*)? The familiar Pauline distinction between "wisdom" and "foolishness" in this passage is not a rigid binary that implies some sort of moral choice or life policy. Stylistically speaking, it amounts to the kind of dialectical reversal for which Paul is famous and which inspired the great Swiss theologian Karl Barth almost a century ago in his *Epistle to the Romans* to pronounce a grand *Nein,* or "no," on all declarative statements or claims to settled knowledge that the intellectual legacy of the West (the "word of man") had always held dear.

But Paul is saying something even more radical that is all too frequently missed in the routine devotional use of this particular passage. He is saying that wisdom in the classic sense of a general theoretical understanding of how things fit together, carefully derived through argument and demonstration as philosophers are accustomed to doing, totally shatters against the reality of the crucified God. In addition, the "foolish" are not the ignorant, but those who never bought into the pretension that to know what we need to know we are obliged to proceed by such rigorous and disciplined discourse, which often turns out to be "sophistical," the cheap substitute for *sophia*, or "wisdom," itself. Genuine knowledge is *existential knowledge*, which means that it is not in the final analysis about things, or the nature of things, but about what ultimately matters to you and I. It is, as the passage above indicates, a "message" (*kerygma*) that is "preached to those who believe," or those who respond positively with their whole being.

The message preached, of course, as Paul emphasizes in the final sentence of this set of passages, is "Christ crucified." The "epistemological" content of Paul's statement—i.e., the kind of "knowledge" it constitutes or connotes—is something that conventional theological discourse has tended to slight or slide by. On the main the Western theological tradition has followed the sort of reading to which the second to third century church father Tertullian gave currency—that death of God on the Cross is incapable of conceptual assimilation, or theological accommodation. *Cria quia absurdum,* "I believe because it is absurd," Tertullian is most famous for declaring alongside his well-known remark about Athens and Jerusalem. But the expression "Christ crucified" is not simply the nub of some theological affirmation that can be contended for, debated, or rounded out in terms of the criteria operative in propositional logic (which Tertullian rightly ascertained is ridiculous from the outset). Its singularity as an unfamiliar "epistemic" principle can be discerned in the last sentence. Jews "ask for signs" and "Greeks search for wisdom." But neither of those alternative should be considered in even the remotest manner adequate to make sense of that incomparable and irreducible event we know as the crucifixion of God, or more popularly the "death of God."

Thus when Rodkey preaches "the death of God" he is doing nothing more or less than what Paul himself demanded. In fact, such a "message," as scholars have pointed out, was fairly standard among the early Christian evangelists themselves.[2] It was this message of "the messiah (*Christos*) crucified" turned totally on its head the customary, worldly associations of divinity, political supremacy, and power. Christ in this sense is no longer the recognizable Greek *sophia*, God's "wisdom," verse 24 tells us, but God's "power" (*dynamis*). The free association between knowledge, wisdom, and power was at the heart of the ancient view of things, and it was revived centuries later during the Renaissance as the anchor assumption of early modernity and the quest for scientific certainty. We find this idea epitomized in Sir Francis Bacon's celebrated quip that "knowledge is power." But the death of God—perhaps as the anchor principle of what we have come to refer to as the "postmodern"—resituates power in an entirely different kind of "knowledge."

Paul contrasts Jews and Greeks (or what we recognize as the Athens-Jerusalem binary). Jews want "signs." The Greek *semeia* in this context implies certain miraculous events, like the parting of the Red Sea or the anticipated liberation of the Jewish people from a seemingly all-competent and oppressive Roman *imperium* by a yet undisclosed messianic figure. For the Greeks, it is not miracles but *sophia*, or sound reasoning. However, neither side of this dichotomy—the dichotomy, which in fact, throughout the ages has been posed by thinkers as the essential tension of the theological undertaking itself, as the give and take between "faith" and "reason"—is sufficient when we are confronted with Christ on the cross.

What do we encounter when we come up in the Gospels to something other than this all-too-often-invoked dichotomy? The philosopher Nietzsche understood quite well that the dichotomy was a false one, and that it was much too frequently used as a Hobson's choice that masked a profound form of cultural decadence and a shameless intellectual dishonesty. Those, like myself, who are not only Nietzsche scholars, but are apt to take with a grain of salt Nietzsche's own tirades against Paul whom he regarded as the source of everything that is wrong with Christianity, recognize that the prophet of "God's death" ironically discerned that something was missing all along in the way "theologians" formulated the very insight that came to a Pharisee from Tarsus as it occurs in the aforementioned passage from Corinthians.

The entirety of Nietzsche's critique of Christianity (which interestingly excludes Jesus, who he named the "only true Christian") turns on the insight that it is not a form of knowledge at all, even knowledge of God, but a secret rage for punishment and a thirst for revenge that dresses itself up as a type of superior morality based on some allegedly transcendent grasp of that which really is. This underlying human drive, which he sarcastically termed the "will to truth," deploys as its instrument of torment the Greek metaphysical claim that we can reason to the cause of things, to "first principles," to Plato's unassailable *eidos*, or "face" (the more proper way of rendering what is popularly translated as "form"), of absolute truth under the name of the Good, or even of *God*.

Christianity transfers to this closet moral imperative, resembling in many ways the Law in Paul that can never be satisfied by human striving, the Greek authority of *epistemic certainty*, the indubitable knowledge—as Descartes would later characterize it—of "first things." The tendency of Christianity to transform what Nietzsche termed its deep-seated attitude of "resentment" against life itself into an actual "ontology," a set of non-negotiable claims about the ultimate order of things, is a force that results not only in fanaticism and dogmatism, but a momentum toward exclusion, persecution, and even sadistic cruelty as evidenced in the record of the Inquisition. It is this perverse use, as Nietzsche maintained, of the concept of Greek "wisdom" to enforce a set of life-denying values and to empower the spirit of resentment and revenge that led him to describe Christianity as "Platonism for the mob."

Furthermore, it is this disguised spirit of death and death-dealing in Christianity that undergirds Nietzsche's announcement through the parable of the madman in the marketplace of God's death. Our many so-called "death of God theologians," in pronouncing the divine demise as a joyful event of secular emancipation, misread the parable in one absolutely critical respect. They overlook the portion of the parable, as well as its more disturbing implications, that the death of God is the consequence of a collective act of Deicide. "We have killed him, you and I. All of us are his murderers."[3] Both Jews and Greeks are responsible for this unspeakable violence on the part of the finite against the Infinite. The crucifixion of the Son of God is the grand historical testimony to the fact that little minds of little men and women cannot bear the reality of a God who is not a subterfuge for our collective egotistical pretensions and narcissistic fantasies of power, but one who utterly shatters, as Paul writes, "the wisdom of the wise." Therefore, we may speak of the "death of God" as a double reading concerning the meaning of the phrase as both a Nietzschean exposé of the corporate motives of historical Christianity and the "moronic pathology" (a more vigorous translation of the New Testament Greek word usually rendered as "foolishness") manifesting in everything from conventional wisdom to philosophical and even "scientific" understanding.

It is this manner of interpreting the phrase "death of God" that takes us in the direction of the kind of radical gospel messaging to be teased from Rodkey's preaching. The idea of a crucified God necessitates a crucified world, a "world as crucifixion," because everyday reality as we are wont to experience it is not "really real." In fact, everyday reality is what the French philosopher Jean Baudrillard has dubbed the "hyperreal," a real that is "more real than real" because it is nothing more than a processions of ideal constructs and airy signifiers that we take to be real because they are the way we want the world to be, or desire to be. Our psychic machinery of desire, as the psychoanalyst Jacques Lacan emphasized, is constantly generating this ideal (or hyperreal) script which we construe as the real itself, what he named the "symbolic order."

We are locked into this relentless shadow play of words, mistaken as things, and it is only when the script comes unraveled and garbled in the act of performance that we are troubled. Most of the time we become angry, and blame it on something, or someone else, even God. It is, however, according to Lacan at this juncture of disruption that we come to "realize" the Real as something that intrudes on our sense of pseudo-reality, on our comfortable symbolic habits and attachments, as a kind of "transcendental" unity of genuine and powerful knowledge that only arises in the anguish of our existential dilemma, when we are up against the possibility of death, meaninglessness, or non-being, or are all too cognizant of rampant suffering and injustice. Such knowledge is what Paul later in his writings referred to as a kind of sudden, or *event-like,* knowledge. The Greek word here is *epignosis,* suggesting the kind of unanticipated knowledge that arises from a conversion, or conversion-like encounter. This is the kind of knowledge that only "Christ" can give us, not Christ in glory, but "Christ crucified."

If the "world" (*kosmos* in Greek) is this unrecognized shadow play of a real that is not really real, but only a mask for resentment, it is therefore a colossal projection of what Paul dubbed the "old nature" which we must be replaced that is the "new nature" that is our nature once we are a "new Being" in Christ. It is the purpose of preaching, therefore, to reverse the symbolic order, even if that order is thoroughly informed and infused with "good Christian" theological precepts about how to live life. For the only "message," or *kerygma,* that counts is that of the world crucified through Christ, in other words, "God's death." Rodkey writes in his introduction: "Radical preaching, then, is an act of reversing the reversals, of exposing and illuminating the reversals which need to be reversed. Telling stories, reciting songs and poetry, interpreting sacred texts which aid and inspire the reversal of reversals. The act of reversing reversals." In his own preaching Jesus was the master of communicating these reversals—from the story of the rich young man to the parable of the talents.

The central motif of Jesus' preaching, the Kingdom of God, is one of absolute reversal, where the first are last, and the last are first. What Nietzsche denominated as the "Christian moral view of the world," which has dominated the outlook of Christendom since the closure of the apostolic age, must now be reversed through radical thinking, radical theologizing, radical philosophizing, radical action, and—most importantly—a radical "preaching" or proclamation that demands that the mask of the world itself be torn off.

—Carl A. Raschke

# Notes

Foreword

1. Friedrich Nietzsche, *The Gay Science*, trans. W. Kaufmann (New York: Vintage, 1974), 125.

2. Isaiah 43:19 (NRSV).

3. John Caputo, *The Insistence of God: A Theology of Perhaps* (Bloomington, IN: Indiana UP, 2014), 230.

Introduction

1. Thomas J. J. Altizer, "The End" (letter), 14. November 2014.

2. Pope Benedict XVI, *Jesus Christ through the Eyes of Pope Benedict XVI*, ed. Giuliano Vigni (Washington, DC: US Conference on Catholic Bishops, 2012), quoted in *Heart to Heart: A Tribute to His Holiness, Pope Francis* (Latrobe, PA: St. Vincent Archabbey, 2013), 7.

3. Gabriel Vahanian, *Theopoetics of the Word* (New York: Palgrave, 2014), 121.

4. Christopher Rodkey, *Too Good To Be True* (Winchester, UK: Christian Alternative, 2014).

5. Thomas Altizer, *The Gospel of Christian Atheism* (Philadelphia: Westminster, 1966), 152.

6. Acts 2.

7. Cf. D. G. Leahy, *Foundation* (Albany, NY: SUNY, 1995), 146.

8. William Blake, in "Jerusalem."

9. Matthew 17:20.

10. Matthew 5:3-12 and Luke 6:20.

11. Cf. Mary Daly, *Pure Lust* (Boston: Beacon, 1984).

12. Cf. Mary Daly and Jane Caputi, *Webster's First New Intergalactic Wickedary of the English Language* (Boston: Beacon, 1987).

13. Richard Swanson, *Provoking the Gospel of Matthew* (Cleveland, Pilgrim, 2007), *Provoking the Gospel of Mark* (Cleveland: Pilgrim, 2005), *Provoking the Gospel of Luke* (Cleveland: Pilgrim, 2006), and *Provoking the Gospel of John* (Cleveland: Pilgrim, 2010).

14. Congregational Vitality and Discipleship Ministry Team of the Local Church Ministries of the United Church of Christ, "SAMUEL: Preaching in the United Church of Christ," online, accessible at http://www.ucc.org/worship/samuel.

15. Paul Nuechterlein, ed. and comp., "Girardian Reflections on the

Lectionary," online, accessible at http://girardianlectionary.net.

16. *An und für sich*, online, http://itself.wordpress.com.

Palm Sunday in December

1. Qur'an, Sura 19, verses 16-36, taken from Nicolas Starkovsky's *The Koran Handbook: An Annotated Translation* (New York: Algora, 2005), 249-250.

2. As per Sura 19.

Come, Lord Jesus

1. This sermon was inspired by Catherine Keller's *The Cloud of Impossibility* (Columbia UP, 2014) and John Vest's sermon, "Who Are You?", Adventures in Postmodernism, online, accessed 20. December 2014.

2. Genesis 1:1ff.

3. Exodus 10:21-22.

4. Mark 15:33, Luke 23:44-45; 1 Peter 3:19-20. Darkness is also an important theme throughout the book of Amos.

Crib Notes from Bethlehem

1. I have cribbed this title from Laurel Schneider's excellent essay of the same title, "Crib Notes from Bethlehem" in *Polydoxy: Theology of Multiplicity and Relation* (New York: Routledge, 2011): 19-35.

Coyote Gospel

1. See Peter Rollins, "What Happens When You Get What You Want?", accessed online, 8. January 2012.

2. "Road Runner Hershey's Commercial 1986," DailyMotion, accessed 8. January 2012.

When Atheists Come for Pizza

1. This all took place in Lebanon, Pennsylvania, in late January and early February, 2010.

Why I Should Be Pope

1. Matthew 23.

2. Gil Bailie, Girardian Commentary on the Lectionary, online, accessed 15. September 2014.

Smelling Like Pig Slop and Loose Women

1. *Pinocchio*, dir. Ben Sharpsteen and Hamilton Luske (Walt Disney Productions, 1940).

2. *Finding Nemo*, dir. Andrew Stanton (Walt Disney Pictures/Pixar

Animation Studios, 2003).

3. Anne Howard, "Prodigal Welcome," The Beatitudes Society, online, accessed 15. September 2014.

The Resurrectionist

1. Sarah Wise, *The Italian Boy: A Tale of Murder and Body Snatching in1830s London* (New York: Metropolitan Books, 2004). I come to this text, and the title of the sermon, through the Pet Shop Boys song, "The Resurrectionist," which is about the history of resurrectionists in England (found on *Format*, EMI [2012]).

2. Sirach 24:7.

3. John 19:39. This is further unpacked in another sermon, "Nicodemus' Secret," which appeared in *Too Good to Be True*, p. 96-100.

4. See Exodus 25, 30, 35; Leviticus 16:12-13; and 1 Chronicles 28:18, 2:4 and 2 Chronicles 13:11.

5. Wikipedia, quoted from Andrew Dalby, "Spikenard" in Alan Davidson, *The Oxford Companion to Food*, 2nd ed. by Tom Jaine (Oxford: Oxford University Press, 2006).

6. See Nietzsche's declaration of the death of God in *The Gay Science*, 125, and discussed in the introductory essay in my *Too Good to Be True* (Winchester, UK: Christian Alternative, 2014), 5-24.

7. Cf. Thomas J. J. Altizer, *The Call to Radical Theology*, ed. Lissa McCullough (Albany, NY: SUNY, 2012), 51ff.

How We Kill God

1. Much of my interpretation of the story of John 8:1-11 and Appolnius of Tana is taken from René Girard, *I See Satan Fall Like Lightning* (New York: Orbis, 2001), chapter 4.

The World is Crucifixion

1. *America's Hardest Prisons*, also known as *Lockdown*, prod. Gail Mitchell.

2. Malcolm X, *The Autobiography of Malcolm X* (New York: Grove, 1965).

3. See Simcha Weinstein, *Up, Up, and Oy Vey!* (Baltimore, Leviathan, 2006).

Some Gods Must Die

1. Girardian Commentary on the Lectionary, accessed at http://girardianlectionary.net/year_a/proper_8a_2011_ser.htm.

2. Søren Kierkegaard, *Fear and Trembling*, trans. W. Lowrie (Princeton: Princeton UP, 1941).

I Believe in the Insurrection!

1. This sermon is inspired by Peter Rollins' *Insurrection* (New York, Howard), 2011.

2. Peter Rollins, Insurrection videos, YouTube.

3. From Jeremiah Wright, speech at Lancaster Theological Seminary, 2013.

Open Hearts, Open Minds, Rigor Mortis

1. Ezra 1:2.

The Courage to Blaspheme

1. Nikos Kazantzakis, *The Last Temptation of Christ* (New York: Simon and Schuster, 1960); and its film, dir. Martin Scorsese (1989).

2. Søren Kierkegaard, *Attack Upon "Christendom,"* trans. W. Lowrie (Boston: Beacon, 1956).

Why You Should Work on the Sabbath

1. Acts 2.

2. John 5:17.

3. Swanson, *Provoking the Gospel of Luke*, 183-4

4. Some ideas from this sermon are taken from the Girardian Commentary on the lectionary, http://girardianlectionary.net/year_c/proper16c.htm.

You Can Take It With You!

1. Joke from http://www.stromer.com/jokes/185jokes.html.

2. From the Girardian Commentary on the Lectionary.

Afterword

1. 1 Corinthians 1:18-23 (NASB).

2. See Paul Ellingworth and Howard Hatton, *A Translator's Handbook on Paul's First Letter to the Corinthians* (New York: United Bible Societies, 1985).

3. Nietzsche, *The Gay Science*, 125.

Made in the USA
Middletown, DE
30 June 2016